JESUS
ON LEADERSHIP

Becoming a Servant Leader

C. GENE WILKES

LifeWay Press®
Nashville, Tennessee

© 1996 LifeWay Press® • Revised 1998, 2015

No part of this book may be reproduced or transmitted in any form or by any means, electronic or mechanical, including photocopying and recording, or by any information storage or retrieval system, except as may be expressly permitted in writing by the publisher. Requests for permission should be addressed in writing to LifeWay Press®; One LifeWay Plaza; Nashville, TN 37234-0152.

ISBN 978-1-4158-6512-5 • Item 005126525
Dewey decimal classification: 303.3 • Subject heading: LEADERSHIP

Cover: Jesus Washing Peter's Feet (engraving), English School, (19th century) / Private Collection / © Look and Learn / Bridgeman Images

Unless indicated otherwise, Scripture quotations are taken from the Holman Christian Standard Bible®, Copyright © 1999, 2000, 2002, 2003, 2009 by Holman Bible Publishers. Used by permission. Holman Christian Standard Bible®, Holman CSB®, and HCSB® are federally registered trademarks of Holman Bible Publishers. Scripture quotations marked NIV are taken from the Holy Bible, NEW INTERNATIONAL VERSION®. Copyright © 1973, 1978, 1984 by Biblica Inc. All rights reserved worldwide. Used by permission. Scripture quotations marked NASB are taken from the New American Standard Bible®, Copyright © 1960, 1962, 1963, 1968, 1971, 1972, 1973, 1975, 1977, 1995 by The Lockman Foundation. Used by permission. (www.lockman.org). Scripture quotations marked KJV are taken from the King James Version.

To order additional copies of this resource, write to LifeWay Resources Customer Service; One LifeWay Plaza; Nashville, TN 37234-0113; fax 615.251.5933; call toll free 800.458.2772; order online at www.lifeway.com; email orderentry@lifeway.com; or visit the LifeWay Christian Store serving you.

Printed in Canada

Groups Ministry Publishing • LifeWay Resources • One LifeWay Plaza • Nashville, TN 37234-0152

Contents

The Author

 C. Gene Wilkes is the president and a professor of New Testament and Leadership at B. H. Carroll Theological Institute in Irving, Texas. Dr. Wilkes embraces the institute's mission to "equip men and women called to serve Christ in the diverse and global ministries of His church." He has written 11 books, including *Jesus on Leadership: Timeless Wisdom on Servant Leadership* and *A New Way of Living: Practicing the Beatitudes Every Day.* Dr. Wilkes received his PhD in New Testament Studies and his MDiv from Southwestern Baptist Theological Seminary. He graduated from Baylor University with a bachelor of arts in religion and Greek.

Dr. Wilkes served as the senior pastor of Legacy Church in Plano, Texas, for 26 years prior to coming to Carroll Institute as the vice president of development. During his local-church ministry, Legacy Church transitioned to become a mission outpost where every member was a missionary in his or her mission field.

Dr. Wilkes has also taught biblical servant leadership as an adjunct professor in the Gary Cook School of Leadership at Dallas Baptist University at both the master's and doctoral levels. Along with his teaching ministry, Dr. Wilkes speaks nationally and internationally on the topic of servant leadership and as a Bible teacher. Some of the international sites include Mexico, Cuba, China, Vietnam, Albania, Greece, Russia, Canada, Portugal, and Honduras.

Dr. Wilkes lives in Plano, Texas, with his wife, Kim, and they have two married daughters and two grandchildren. Dr. Wilkes's hobbies include trail running, hiking, mountaineering, cycling, and golf. He summited 14,410-foot Mount Rainier, Washington, on his 60th birthday in 2013.

Introduction

Jesus on Leadership: Becoming a Servant Leader originated in a local church setting and, since its first printing in 1998, has continued to provide direction and aid to churches worldwide. This Bible study attempts to develop leaders by following the pattern of Jesus' ministry of training people to do Kingdom work. Although the study is neither the first nor the last word in leadership discovery and development in the church, developing servant leaders is what the church has been about since Jesus affirmed Peter's confession of faith and established His church on that rock. Training servant leaders will be a task of the church until Christ returns.

Jesus on Leadership joins many books about leadership in church and business. Interest and materials about servant leadership have grown in both secular and ministry contexts. More needs to be written and modeled to provide service-first leadership among God's people. Too many works start with characteristics of a leader and then, if at all, move to Jesus' life and teachings to support those ideas. This workbook starts with the ways Jesus modeled and taught leadership, then brings principles gleaned from His ministry into church life. The challenge is to make Jesus' example the guide and focus of leadership among God's people. As long as church members revere a worldly model of leadership more than Jesus' examples and teaching, misunderstanding and conflict will result. In contrast, when a church follows a biblical model of servant leadership for all its leaders, God works in amazing ways through those leaders. That's my prayer for your church.

"Every generous act and every perfect gift is from above" (Jas. 1:17). I acknowledge God's hand in the entire process of completing this project. I want to thank Henry Webb for his initial trust in me and his encouragement throughout this project. I worked closely with Sam House and Richard Ryan during the production stage, and I thank them for their diligence and attention to detail. I'm also grateful to the people who are Legacy Church in Plano, Texas, where I was the senior pastor for 26 years. Their vision and mission to make disciples created the environment for such a study.

My wife, Kim, is my best friend. Without her support throughout my writing and sharing this message, I couldn't have completed this project. And to my daughters, who put up with Daddy's writing habits, I say a very special "Thank you."

May this workbook guide you and your church to discover and develop servant leaders. May God use this Bible study "for the training of the saints in the work of ministry, to build up the body of Christ" (Eph. 4:12).

CORE CONCEPTS OF SERVANT LEADERSHIP

SERVANT LEADERS SERVE GOD AND EQUIP OTHERS FOR TEAM MINISTRY

God Prepares Servant Leaders to **SERVE**

SPIRITUAL GIFTS

EXPERIENCES

RELATIONAL STYLE

VOCATIONAL SKILLS

ENTHUSIASM

Servant Leaders **EQUIP** *Others*

ENCOURAGE THEM TO SERVE.

QUALIFY THEM FOR SERVICE.

UNDERSTAND THEIR NEEDS.

INSTRUCT THEM.

PRAY FOR THEM.

Servant Leaders Serve in **TEAM** *Ministry*

TOGETHERNESS

EMPOWERMENT

ACCOUNTABILITY

MENTORING

Biblical Principles of Servant Leadership

1. Servant leaders humble themselves and wait for God to exalt them (see Luke 14:7-11).
2. Servant leaders follow Jesus rather than seek a position (see Mark 10:32-40).
3. Servant leaders give up personal rights to find greatness in service to others (see Mark 10:41-45).
4. Servant leaders can risk serving others because they trust that God is in control of their lives (see John 13:3).
5. Servant leaders take up Jesus' towel of servanthood to meet the needs of others (see John 13:4-11).
6. Servant leaders share their responsibility and authority with others to meet a greater need (see Acts 6:1-6).
7. Servant leaders multiply their leadership by empowering others to lead (see Ex. 18:17-23).

Week 1

DOWN FROM THE
HEAD TABLE

This Week's Memory Verse

Even the Son of Man did not come to be served,
but to serve, and to give His life—a ransom for many.
MARK 10:45

One day I found myself at the head table at a typical denominational event. As the leader of the church-growth team, I was responsible for introducing the speaker. Others sitting at the head table included the director of missions, the moderator, the person singing the special music and her spouse, and the speaker. After I'd introduced the speaker, everyone at the head table stood and moved to sit in the audience—everyone but me! The speaker, noticing that the others were leaving the head table, said, "If you're at the head table and would like to move, you may at this time." Alone, I stood and said, "I'd love to!" We all laughed, and I walked red-faced to sit at a table with those who served in the kitchen.

As the blood gradually returned to the rest of my body, Jesus' story about where to sit at big meals came to mind. At the home of a prominent Pharisee, He taught the people:

When you are invited by someone to a wedding banquet, don't recline
at the best place, because a more distinguished person than you
may have been invited by your host. The one who invited both of you
may come and say to you, "Give your place to this man," and then in
humiliation, you will proceed to take the lowest place. But when you
are invited, go and recline in the lowest place, so that when the one
who invited you comes, he will say to you, "Friend, move up higher."
You will then be honored in the presence of all the other guests.
LUKE 14:8-10

As I reflected on my social blunder, I realized I'd done what was typical of many leaders. When given a position, we happily accept the status that goes with it, often overlooking the fact that the true place of Christlike leadership is out in the crowd rather than at the head table. Leaders who follow Christ's model of leadership work with those who serve in the kitchen and serve alongside them until they complete the job. Head tables are optional. Service, not status, is the goal of leaders who have Christ as their master.

Many churches and ministries struggle because they lack servant leaders. Head tables have replaced the towel and washbasin as symbols of leadership among God's people. Churches and ministries, however, need leaders who know how God has made and gifted them for service and who serve Christ's mission of reconciliation. Churches need leaders who have the skills to equip others to team with them in ministry. Churches need leaders who will step down from the head table and be willing to serve in the kitchen. Churches today need men and women who will stop following the world's concepts of leadership and adopt Jesus' teachings and example of servant leadership.

The term *servant leadership* isn't an oxymoron![1] Neither is the word *servant* a soft-shell cover for what leadership really is. *Servant* and *leader* stand together as a model for people called to influence others to work toward the mission of God. Leadership through service is the way Jesus modeled and taught discipleship among His followers. True servant leadership begins by submitting to Jesus and obediently following His teachings and lifestyle. You can lead like Jesus only when you obey His teachings about leading as a servant.

Jesus was a servant leader. He was a servant to the Father's mission, and He was a servant to those on mission with Him. His model provides the basis for our working definition of *servant leader*:

> A servant leader serves the mission and leads
> by serving those on mission with Him.[2]

This study will help churches discover, equip, and place servant leaders in all areas of ministry. Jesus' teachings and model of servant leadership are the foundation for this study. Participants will discover their roles as servant leaders and will be equipped for team ministry. Our purpose as individual members, as a church, or as a ministry is to develop servant leaders in team ministry who carry out the mission of God. My prayer is that churches and ministries will honor and train leaders who follow Jesus' teachings and model of servant leadership. My personal goal is to serve you and your church through this Bible study and to help restore a biblical model of servant leadership in your church.

This Week You Will

- Discover seven principles of servant leadership (days 1–4).
- Examine definitions of *servant leadership* and Jesus' teachings about humility (day 1).
- Examine Jesus' teachings about being first and being great (day 2).
- Observe Jesus' model of servant leadership the night He was betrayed (day 3).
- Examine biblical models of shared leadership (day 4).
- Evaluate God's calling in your life to be a servant leader (day 5).

1. An oxymoron is a figure of speech that combines opposite or contradictory ideas or terms. Examples are "civil war" and "bittersweet."
2. C. Gene Wilkes, *Jesus on Leadership: Discovering the Secrets of Servant Leadership from the Life of Christ* (Carol Stream, IL: Tyndale, 1998), 18.

Day 1
JESUS' TEACHINGS ON LEADERSHIP, PART 1

Christian leaders are servants with credibility and capabilities, who are able to influence people in a particular context to pursue their God-given direction.[1]
AUBREY MALPHURS

Today You Will
- Review the biblical concept of servant leadership.
- Examine Jesus' teachings about humility.
- Take inventory of your relationship with Jesus Christ.
- Study Jesus' model of humble service to all.

Today we want to examine different ideas about leadership. We'll look at biblical models of leadership and the ways Jesus taught and modeled leadership for His followers. Let's start with your impressions of a leader.

Below you'll find a list of character traits. Select the qualities you consider important in a leader.

Honesty	Kindness	Fairness	Goal-oriented
Humility	Boldness	Caring	Integrity
Godliness	Above average	Serving	Inspiring
Dependability	Emotional	Decisive	Cautious
Cooperative	Independent	Loyal	Intelligent

Return to the list and circle the characteristics that are present in your life.

People know what they want in a leader. Some prefer that their leader be decisive or visionary. Others want their leader to be charming and kind to people. Some desire not to have a leader!

I want to highlight the trait of service in a leader. Such a leader serves the mission and meets the needs of the group that relate to the group's goals. This kind of leader leads by example rather than by memo.

In 1977 Robert Greenleaf, who was then an executive in the communications industry and is best known for making popular the concept of servant leadership, announced to the world that a new moral principle was emerging in society. He wrote that in the future "the only truly viable institutions will be those that are predominately servant-led."[2]

Observing that people respond best to leaders who are servants to the group or institution, Greenleaf called for servant-led organizations. He understood that people had lost an appetite for bosses who lord it over them. People prefer to follow those who help them, not those who intimidate them.

J. Oswald Sanders, whose book *Spiritual Leadership* has become a classic, wrote:

> True greatness, true leadership, is achieved not by reducing men to one's service but in giving oneself in selfless service to them. And this is never done without cost. … The true spiritual leader is concerned infinitely more with the service he can render God and his fellowmen than with the benefits and pleasures he can extract from life. He aims to put more into life than he takes out of it.[3]

Sanders and Greenleaf call for the same quality in a leader: a servant's heart. This mark of a leader isn't a new discovery. It's an affirmation of Jesus' teachings on leadership. Sanders's source for his description of leadership is Jesus' teachings. He found true leadership in Jesus' examples of and teaching about being a servant.

Leadership in the kingdom of God is different from leadership in the world. It's still leadership, an individual who influences others toward a shared goal, but those who lead in the kingdom of God look very different from those who lead by the world's standards. Life under the lordship of Christ has different values from life under the lordship of self. Therefore, kingdom leaders are people who lead like Jesus. They act differently from leaders trained by the world. Kingdom leaders are servant leaders because they follow Jesus, who "did not come to be served, but to serve" (Mark 10:45).

Jesus taught His disciples a valuable lesson about head tables and a humble spirit.

Jesus' Story About Humility

Read Luke 14:1,7-11. Where was Jesus when He told this story (see v. 1)?

Why did He tell the story (see v. 7)?

Put yourself in the disciples' sandals. What would your response be to Jesus' message in that place to those people?

Jesus told this story to His followers while they attended a meal at the house of a prominent religious leader. Noticing that the guests picked places of honor at the head table near the host, Jesus chose this situation to teach His disciples how they should behave toward places of honor.

Write the main point of each verse in the parable.

Verse 8:

Verse 9:

Verse 10:

Verse 11:

Jesus said those who follow Him must first humble themselves. Any head-table recognition should come from others. Final recognition will come from God. The world says, "Take a seat at the head table." Jesus says, "Take a seat at the back. I'll choose who sits up front."

The word *humble* in verse 11 means to "make low or humiliate by assigning to a low(er) place."[4] Jesus called His disciples to lower themselves rather than exalt themselves. He made it clear that His followers weren't to seek places of honor. Jesus' disciples wait for their Host to invite them to the head table. They don't seek high places on their own. The Bible says, "Humility comes before honor" (Prov. 15:33). Moses was more humble "than any man on the face of the earth" (Num. 12:3). His life demonstrated that humility is the confidence you lead by God's choosing rather than by your efforts, and with this certainty you can even take up for those who are trying to take your place (see the rest of the story in Num. 12).

SERVANT LEADERSHIP PRINCIPLE 1
Servant leaders humble themselves and wait for God to exalt them.

Those Jesus calls to lead willingly humble themselves to God's mission call on their lives and patiently wait for Him to direct them to positions of leadership in His timing.

Humility, not pride, is the hallmark of a servant leader's character. Patience, not aggressiveness, illustrates a servant leader's dependence on God rather than himself.

You can't apply this first principle of a servant leader to your life unless you commit yourself to follow Jesus' teachings. You must decide whether you'll pattern your life after the model of Jesus or around the thinking and experience of the world.

Before we go any further, you must settle this issue in your life. You must answer the question, Who's the Master of my life? Here's why your answer to that question is basic to this study: no one can be a servant without a master. You can't be a servant leader as modeled by Jesus without having Him as your Master. Jesus said:

> No one can be a slave of two masters, since either he will hate one
> and love the other, or be devoted to one and despise the other.
> **MATTHEW 6:24**

Leaders without Jesus as their Master can serve only themselves, not others.

Take a moment to examine your heart and answer the following questions.

Have I confessed my sinfulness and resistance to God's leadership in my life?   Yes   No

Have I confessed that Jesus is the Lord of my life (see Rom. 10:9)? Yes   No

Do I live my life as if I am in control or as if Christ is in control (see Gal. 2:20)?   I am.   Christ is.

Do I show a willingness to humble myself before others, or am I happier when I earn a seat at a head table?   I humble myself. I love earning my seat.

The answers to these questions characterize your relationship with Jesus Christ. The rest of this workbook will be only an exercise in self-will if Christ isn't in control of every aspect of your life. If you want to settle this issue in your life right now, pause and ask Christ to be the Savior and Lord of your life. Then call your group's leader or your pastor and ask this person to join you in prayer. Be prepared to share your decision at the next group session.

An Attitude like Jesus

The apostle Paul asked the Christians in Philippi to serve one another the way Jesus would serve them. Paul reminded his friends of their source of strength, fellowship, and unity in Christ. He wrote, "Make your own attitude that of Christ Jesus" (Phil. 2:5). Paul then described Jesus' humble service of taking on the form of a man and dying on the cross for others.

As you read Philippians 2:5-11, underline words that describe the ways Jesus humbled Himself. Then go through the verses again and circle words that indicate the way God exalted Jesus.

Make your own attitude that of Christ Jesus,
who, existing in the form of God,
did not consider equality with God
as something to be used for His own advantage.
Instead He emptied Himself
by assuming the form of a slave,
taking on the likeness of men.
And when He had come as a man
in His external form,
He humbled Himself by becoming obedient
to the point of death—
even to death on a cross.
For this reason God highly exalted Him
and gave Him the name
that is above every name,
so that at the name of Jesus
every knee will bow—
of those who are in heaven and on earth
and under the earth—
and every tongue should confess
that Jesus Christ is Lord,
to the glory of God the Father.
PHILIPPIANS 2:5-11

The key phrase in the first half of this passage is "He humbled Himself" (v. 8). Paul's term for *humble* is the same word Jesus used in His story to the disciples in Luke 14:7-11. Jesus taught humility because it was at the core of who He was. It was God's plan for His Son's life. The key phrase in the second half of Philippians 2:5-11 is "God highly exalted Him" (v. 9). Paul's word for *exalt* is also the same word Jesus used in His story in Luke. God exalted His Son after Jesus humbled Himself in obedience to death on the cross. Peter, who was present when Jesus taught this lesson about humility, later told the early Christians to "humble yourselves, therefore, under the mighty hand of God, so that He may exalt you at the proper time" (1 Pet. 5:6).

Servant leaders in the church humble themselves in obedience to Christ. Exaltation is God's choice, not ours. Leaders must have the humble spirit of Christ and must be willing to take the seats at the back. God will choose those who will sit up front.

PERSONAL REVIEW

Prayerfully take time to consider your answers to the following questions.

Am I trusted as a leader because people see me as a servant?
Yes   No

Am I willing to wait for the invitation of the Host to sit at the head table?   Yes   No

Do people see the humility of Christ in my life?   Yes   No

Is Jesus genuinely the Master of my life?   Yes   No

Am I willing to humble myself like Jesus to allow God to accomplish His plan for my life?   Yes   No

PRINCIPLES OF SERVANT LEADERSHIP

Principle 1: Servant leaders _____ themselves and wait for God to _____ them.

SUMMARY

- Servant leadership principle 1: Servant leaders humble themselves and wait for God to exalt them.
- True leadership begins with a servant's heart.
- Jesus taught His disciples not to seek places at the head table.
- Jesus must be your Master before you can be a servant leader like Him.
- Jesus modeled a servant's heart in His incarnation and in His crucifixion.

1. Aubrey Malphurs, *Being Leaders: The Nature of Authentic Christian Leadership,* Kindle edition (Ada, MI: Baker Publishing Group, 2003), 33.
2. Robert K. Greenleaf, *Servant Leadership* (Mahwah, NJ: Paulist Press, 1977), 10.
3. J. Oswald Sanders, *Spiritual Leadership* (Chicago: Moody Press, 1967), 13.
4. William F. Arndt and Wilbur F. Gingrich, *A Greek-English Lexicon of the New Testament and Other Early Christian Literature* (Chicago: University of Chicago Press, 1957), 812.

Day 2
JESUS' TEACHINGS ON LEADERSHIP, PART 2

Above all, leadership is a position of servanthood.[1]
MAX DEPREE

Today You Will
- Examine James and John's request of Jesus.
- Define greatness and being first as taught by Jesus.
- Discover servant leadership principles 2 and 3.
- Reflect on the biblical event recorded in Mark 10:32-40 and identify ways you can be great and first.

I entered the office of one of our church's volunteers to join him for a lunch meeting. The highly successful salesman was on the phone when I entered his office, so I had time to look around. I checked out his desk to see what mementos or expressions of himself he'd chosen to put there. My eyes immediately went to a message on his desk. It read, "If the meek inherit the earth, what do we tigers get?" I smiled. Later, I realized the sign misrepresented Jesus' teaching on meekness, and it illustrated how many people in our society regard what appears to be weakness in leading others.

Jesus redefined greatness and being first when He declared:

> Whoever wants to become great among you must be your servant,
> and whoever wants to be first among you must be a slave to all.
> **MARK 10:43-44**

You're great when you serve. You're first when you willingly become a slave to the needs of others. Jesus taught this paradox to His closest disciples. These men had accepted Jesus' call to follow Him. They would lead others in His work after Jesus ascended to the right hand of the Father. Their understanding of leadership among God's people was crucial to the way Kingdom people would live together in generations to come.

Jesus taught about greatness and being first after James and John had asked Him a favor. Let's look at what led Jesus to teach His disciples about servant leadership.

James, John, and You

Read Mark 10:32-40. Then answer the following questions.

What did James and John ask Jesus (see v. 37)?

What had Jesus said that caused them to ask the question (see vv. 33-34)?

What was Jesus' reply to their question (see v. 38)?

How did James and John reply to Jesus' comments (see v. 39)?

What did Jesus say to them (see vv. 39-40)?

What do you think of James and John's request?

James and John sensed that something important would happen in Jerusalem. They thought Jesus was getting close to taking His throne, and they selfishly wanted to lead from positions of power beside Him. James and John thought Kingdom leadership meant a position or title. They betrayed their ambitious hearts by being the first among the disciples to make their request of Jesus.

Before you judge the sons of Zebedee, remember that we're very much like them. We too want places up front when Jesus defeats His enemies. We forget, however, that suffering like Jesus comes before reigning with Jesus. Jesus wanted James and John to know that following Him would cost them their lives, not gain them places at the head table. Only the Host knows who sits there.

SERVANT LEADERSHIP PRINCIPLE 2
Servant leaders follow Jesus rather than seek a position.

Following Jesus means setting our personal agendas aside to follow Jesus in obedience. Don Howell Jr. concluded:

New covenant servant-leaders learn, by imitating their servant-Lord, to abandon their own agendas and preferences in order to seek the good of their fellow servants.[2]

Servant leadership isn't about position and power. Leaders among Christ's disciples follow Jesus as He serves others and suffers on their behalf. Servant leadership requires drinking the cup and being baptized with the baptism of Christ's suffering (see vv. 38-39).

The Other 10 Disciples and You

Read Mark 10:41-45. Put yourself in the other 10 disciples' sandals when they heard James and John's request. Answer the following questions.

Were the other disciples' feelings toward James and John justified (see v. 41)?   Yes   No   Why or why not?

When Jesus called the group together, how did He describe the world's concept of leadership (see v. 42)?

Write your own definition of *dominate*.

Write your own definition of *exercise power*.

Jesus said the way the world practices leadership mustn't be the pattern among His true disciples.

Fill in the blanks with Jesus' words in verses 43-44:

Whoever wants to become _____ among you must be your _____,
and whoever wants to be _____ among you must be a _____ to all.
MARK 10:43-44

We get our English prefix *mega* from the Greek word for *great*. Our English word *deacon* comes from the Greek word for *servant*. A servant in the ancient world waited on tables.

Record your understanding of Christlike greatness, based on this information.

We get our English prefix *proto* from the Greek word for *first*. It means *first in a series or line*. No single English word adequately describes the Greek word for *slave (doulos)* in this passage. Such a slave was on the lowest rung of the social ladder. The owner bought and sold slaves like household goods. The *doulos* was a bond slave who served the master without will or question.[3] A slave had no rights or privileges, no wants or desires, only the commands of the master.

Record your understanding of being first among Jesus' disciples, based on this information.

SERVANT LEADERSHIP PRINCIPLE 3
Servant leaders give up personal rights
to find greatness in service to others.

Jesus redefined greatness and being first. He specified the posture required to be a great leader in the mission of God. When you make Jesus Master of your life, you become a servant to others. To lead in the kingdom of God is to serve others and to follow the King.

Jesus, the Servant Leader

Jesus defined greatness as the life of a servant. What does this picture of leadership look like in real life today? How can servants and slaves really lead? The answer poses a real dilemma for a disciple of Jesus.

Servants and slaves don't define *leadership* in the world's dictionary. Many people understand the idea of being a servant and forfeiting personal rights as portraying a negative self-image. Jesus came to show what life in the kingdom of God looks like, not to modify the way the world does things. The ways of God work only in the hallways of humanity when Jesus reigns in our hearts. Any follower of Christ who seeks to lead like Jesus must be willing to be treated like Jesus.

Some will follow. Others will throw stones.

By example Jesus answered the question of how to lead like a servant. He concluded His lesson on leadership:

> Even the Son of Man did not come to be served,
> but to serve, and to give His life—a ransom for many.
> **MARK 10:45**

Jesus wasn't a teacher who merely defined His terms. He also modeled what He called others to do. James, John, and the other 10 disciples experienced what Jesus taught as they followed Him to His death. They soon learned that servant leadership ultimately means giving up oneself so that others can have the life God desires for them.

Jesus deserves service from those He created. However, He came to serve us. He came to give His life as a ransom so that we could be set free from sin. A ransom in the ancient world was a payment to free a slave or prisoner.[4] As the Son of Man, Jesus saw His life as one of sacrifice so that others could benefit.

Jesus is our only true model of servant leadership. He served others by giving His life for them. His entire mission was to free others, not to gain a position for Himself. This is a mystery to the world, but it's the heart of Kingdom leadership. Anyone who seeks to lead in the body of Christ must submit himself or herself to the lordship of Jesus. Only then can we begin to understand why servants are great and slaves are first.

PERSONAL EVALUATION

Jesus responded to the wishes of His disciples and taught them about servant leadership.

Consider your responses to the following statements. Prayerfully record your feelings and thoughts.

I'm like James and John because I ...

I'm like the other 10 disciples because I ...

I can be "great" as a servant this week by ...

I can be "first" as a slave this week by ...

PRINCIPLES OF SERVANT LEADERSHIP

Principle 1: Servant leaders _____ themselves and wait for God to _____ them.

Principle 2: Servant leaders _____ Jesus rather than seek a _____.

Principle 3: Servant leaders give up personal _____ to find greatness in _____ to others.

SUMMARY

- Servant leadership principle 2: Servant leaders follow Jesus rather than seek a position.
- Servant leadership principle 3: Servant leaders give up personal rights to find greatness in service to others.
- Jesus redefined greatness and being first when He declared, "Whoever wants to become great among you must be your servant, and whoever wants to be first among you must be a slave to all" (Mark 10:43-44).
- James and John thought Kingdom leadership meant a position or title.
- Jesus deserves service from all those He created. However, He came not to be served but to serve. He came to give His life as a ransom to free others.

1. Max DePree, *Leadership Jazz* (New York: Dell, 1992), 220.
2. Don N. Howell Jr., *Servants of the Servant* (Eugene, OR: Wipf & Stock Publishers, 2003), 19.
3. Ibid., 6–19. See Howell's description of the biblical words for *servant/slave* and his discussion of this image of God's people and leaders as a significant theme throughout Scripture.
4. William F. Arndt and Wilbur F. Gingrich, *A Greek-English Lexicon of the New Testament and Other Early Christian Literature* (Chicago: University of Chicago Press, 1957), 483.

Day 3
JESUS' MODEL
OF LEADERSHIP

Implicitly, Jesus is saying that leadership in its very essence
is serving. It cannot be otherwise. To lead is to serve. And to
serve is to become the servant of those whom one is leading.[1]
TED ENGSTROM AND PAUL CEDAR

Today You Will
- Discover servant leadership principles 4 and 5.
- Discover the power of servant leadership by examining John's statements
  about Jesus before He washed His disciples' feet.
- Observe that Jesus left His place at the table and washed His disciples' feet.
- Evaluate your feelings as a leader about washing the feet of others.
- Test your knowledge of Jesus' model of servant leadership.

The Power of Servant Leadership

Where do you find the power to serve others? If your ego wars with God for your loyalty,
how can you break the bondage of self-interest to serve those around you? John 13 gives
the account of Jesus' last meal with His disciples. At that meal Jesus modeled for all time
what servant leadership looks like by washing His disciples' feet. John, under the inspira-
tion of the Holy Spirit, noted some details about Jesus before He took up the towel and
basin. These facts reveal the secret to risking servant leadership.

Read John 13:3.

> Jesus knew that the Father had given everything into His hands,
> that He had come from God, and that He was going back to God.
> **JOHN 13:3**

How do you think Jesus' knowledge of these matters influenced His decision to wash the disciples' feet?

Jesus knew His Father "had given everything into His hands." He knew His Father was in control of His life and ministry. He knew His place as the Son of God. Jesus knew "He had come from God." He knew His Father was the source of His mission on earth. He was confident that what He was doing was part of God's ultimate plan for His life. Jesus also knew "He was going back to God." He knew He would return to His eternal place as God in heaven. Jesus' knowledge of these facts, John wrote, preceded His act to take up the towel and basin. Confident of these facts, Jesus was able to model what God had sent Him to do: serve others and lay down His life.

Circle the number that represents your trust in God in the following areas of your life, with 1 being least like you and 5 being most like you.

I trust that in Christ, God has given me power to serve others (see Eph. 2:6-7 for your place in Christ). 1 2 3 4 5
I trust that God created me and has a plan for my life. 1 2 3 4 5
I trust that I will go to be with God at my death. 1 2 3 4 5

These facts of faith are the source of power that allow you to risk leading others as a servant. You're secure enough to brave serving others only when your security is in God and not in yourself. Without God-centered certainty, you have no choice but to protect your ego and defend your rights. Only when you trust God with the absolute control of your life can you risk losing your self and status in service to others.

SERVANT LEADERSHIP PRINCIPLE 4
Servant leaders can risk serving others because
they trust that God is in control of their lives.

Jesus knew His power was from His Father. He knew He came from and was returning to His Father. The secret to risking servant leadership is the assurance that God is in control of your life. Risk is simply the courage to be obedient to God's certain call on a servant leader's life, and "servant leaders are proactive risk takers."[2]

The Ministry of the Towel

I kept a towel in my church office that was stained with shoe polish. I used it when we set apart members of our church as deacons. Each time we did this, I got on my knees and wiped the dust from their shoes in front of the church. I did this for two reasons:

1. To remind myself of my role as their servant leader
2. To remind them of Jesus' example of servant leadership when He washed His disciples' feet

Jesus performed two symbolic acts for His followers on the night He was betrayed. He took up a servant's towel and washbasin and washed their feet. He also took the bread and wine from the Passover meal and announced a new covenant between God and His creation in the blood of Jesus.

When Jesus asked His disciples to prepare the Passover meal, they didn't hire a servant to do the dirty work of washing feet after a day in the dirt of Jerusalem. Instead of scolding them for their incompetence or ordering one of them to do the lowly job, Jesus took up the towel and washbasin because He wanted His closest followers to learn an important lesson that night.

Read John 13:4-11. In your own words, describe what Jesus did.

**When Jesus came to Peter, the fisher of men resisted Jesus.
Why do you think Peter said what he did (see vv. 6,8)?**

How do you relate to what he said?

How did Jesus respond to Peter's resistance (see vv. 7-8)?

Jesus surprised His followers when He left the head table and moved to where servants worked. He took off His outer clothes and picked up a servant's towel. He was now dressed like a servant. He wrapped the towel around His waist, filled a basin with water, and began to wash the dusty feet of His friends. He now did the work of a slave. This wasn't His job. He was Teacher and Lord. Yet Jesus redefined what leaders do: leaders meet the needs of those they lead. Jesus' followers had dirty feet, and no one else was willing to wash them. They had a need, but no one else would leave his place to meet it.

Jesus modeled servant leadership when He willingly left His place at the table and knelt down to meet a need. Peter's response revealed that he didn't get the picture at first. Nobody does. Jesus could only say, "You'll understand later." Jesus' descent from the Passover meal to the servant's towel and washbasin parallels His descent from heaven to the cross (see Phil. 2:5-11). His actions also modeled what He'd taught earlier about being great and first (see Mark 10:35-45). The Teacher modeled in the upper room what He'd taught earlier on the road to Jerusalem. Dressed like a servant and acting like a slave, Jesus led.

SERVANT LEADERSHIP PRINCIPLE 5
Servant leaders take up Jesus' towel of servanthood
to meet the needs of others.

Jesus took the focus off positions and cultural ideas of leadership and placed it on matters of the heart. Reggie McNeal surmised:

> Jesus turned the leadership equation around with his emphasis on servant leadership. Instead of establishing leadership positions in his kingdom, he focused on the character of leadership, declaring it to be that of serving others in humility.[3]

Meeting needs doesn't necessarily mean giving in to people's wishes. Jesus knelt as a servant at Peter's feet, but He didn't allow Peter's personal preference to keep Him from His mission. Peter didn't get his way. Servanthood doesn't mean a lack of resolve or insight. Servants can't waver from doing their master's wishes. Leaders must sometimes reveal a need before meeting it.

Jesus washed the feet of Judas, the disciple who would betray Him with a kiss. Jesus knew Judas would turn Him over to the religious leaders to be crucified, yet He washed his feet. Your greatest test of servant leadership may be to wash the feet of those you know will soon betray you.

Jesus modeled for all what Kingdom leadership looks like. Seeking to lead like Jesus means you must be willing to give up your position in order to serve and kneel at the dirty feet of others. Sometimes that means exposing a need in order to meet it. At other times it means humbling yourself before the ones who will soon turn you over to your enemies.

An Example for All to Follow

Read John 13:12-17.

When Jesus finished washing the disciples' feet, He put on His outer clothes and returned to His place at the table. Having acted out His lesson, He wanted to know whether His students understood (see v. 12).

Jesus said He was His disciples' teacher and master (see v. 13). Because that was true, He said, they must do what He commanded them to do. He said they should "wash one another's feet" (v. 14).

Write some ways you could "wash the feet" of people you know.

Jesus said He set an example for His disciples to follow (see v. 15). The word *example* means "to show under the eyes as an illustration or warning."[4] Jesus modeled behavior He wanted His followers to imitate.

What was the implication of Jesus' words in verses 16?

Jesus concluded His lesson in servant leadership by saying, "As my servants and those whom I've sent, you're to do what I have done." Those who lead in the kingdom of God must check where they sit and what they wear. If you aren't wearing a servant's towel and kneeling at the feet of others, you're in the wrong place.

Those who lead in God's kingdom lead from a kneeling position, dressed like a servant, meeting the needs of those who follow them. Kingdom servant leaders, like Jesus, can dress like a servant, act like a slave, and lead.

Jesus made a promise to His disciples at the end of His lesson. What was it (see v. 17)?

Jesus said you'll receive a blessing when you serve others as He did. God blesses those who take up the towel and washbasin like His Son.

PERSONAL EVALUATION

As you think about what you've learned in today's study, place
a *T* (true) or *F* (false) beside each statement below.

_____ 1. You can be a servant leader by deciding in your own power
to act like Jesus.

_____ 2. You can risk being a servant leader when you trust that God
is in control of your life.

_____ 3. The symbols of Christlike leadership are a towel and a washbasin.

_____ 4. Servant leaders lead from a kneeling position.

_____ 5. Jesus should have honored Peter's request not to wash his feet.

_____ 6. If Jesus led with the towel, so should His followers.

_____ 7. You'll be blessed if you do as Jesus did.

_____ 8. You can serve others when you trust that God is in control
of your life and that God is your beginning and your end.

_____ 9. A leader models servant leadership when he leaves his position
at the head table, takes up tools of service, and kneels at the
feet of others to meet a need.

_____ 10. By His actions on the night He was betrayed, Jesus modeled
what He'd taught about being great and first in Mark 10:35-45.

PRINCIPLES OF SERVANT LEADERSHIP

Principle 1: Servant leaders _____ themselves and wait
for God to _____ them.

Principle 2: Servant leaders _____ Jesus rather than seek
a _____.

Principle 3: Servant leaders give up personal _____ to find
greatness in _____ to others.

Principle 4: Servant leaders can risk serving others because they _____
that God is in _____ of their lives.

Principle 5: Servant leaders take up Jesus' towel of _____
to meet the needs of _____.

SUMMARY

- Servant leadership principle 4: Servant leaders can risk serving others because they trust that God is in control of their lives.
- Servant leadership principle 5: Servant leaders take up Jesus' towel of servanthood to meet the needs of others. Jesus acted out servant leadership by washing His disciples' feet.
- Because Jesus did this for His disciples, you are to do this for those you lead.

Answers to true/false statements: 1. F, 2. T, 3. T, 4. T, 5. F, 6. T, 7. T, 8. T, 9. T, 10. T

1. Theodore Wilhelm Engstrom and Paul A. Cedar, *Compassionate Leadership,* Kindle edition (Ventura, CA: Regal Books, 2006), 814.
2. Aubrey Malphurs, *Being Leaders: The Nature of Authentic Christian Leadership,* Kindle edition (Ada, MI: Baker Publishing Group, 2003), 44.
3. Reggie McNeal, *A Work of Heart: Understanding How God Shapes Spiritual Leaders,* Kindle edition (Hoboken, NJ: Jossey-Bass, 2000), 1261.
4. A. T. Robertson, *Word Pictures in the New Testament,* vol. 5 (Nashville: Sunday School Board of the Southern Baptist Convention, 1932), 240.

Day 4

THEY NEEDED SERVANTS

In *servant* leadership, serving is the expression of leadership, regardless of how people follow. Serving is both the end as well as the means.[1]

STACY T. RINEHART

Today You Will

- Discover how the early church leaders met a pressing ministry need by involving others in leadership.
- Examine Moses' father-in-law's advice to make Moses a more effective leader.
- Understand servant leadership principles 6 and 7.
- Evaluate your role as a servant leader who empowers others to lead with you.

B. H. Carroll was the pastor of First Baptist Church in Waco, Texas, for 29 years, from 1870 to 1899. He saw beyond the needs of his members to the needs of pastors who didn't have theological training. His desire to train future pastors led him to invite students from the newly formed Baylor University into his study to read from his library and to learn from him. He also saw that the need to train pastors and church leaders was far greater than he could meet on his own. His vision led him to enlist others to start a seminary in the southwest that would combine practical application with academic excellence to equip pastors. This pastor and scholar in a local church empowered church leaders through theological education to do the work of Christ for generations to come by recruiting others to join him in equipping church leaders.

A Special Fellowship

After Christ ascended to heaven, He poured out His Spirit on His people at Pentecost. The church grew rapidly. God drew people from all races and walks of life to His church. The new believers lived together in Christian fellowship and shared all they had with one another.

Read Acts 2:42-47. Describe the believers' life together after God poured out His Holy Spirit on them at Pentecost.

In what ways does the church today practice these aspects of Christian fellowship?

Two Threats to Unity

The church in Jerusalem experienced great growth and fellowship through the presence of God's Spirit in people's lives. But as the church grew, two internal cancers threatened to stop the movement of God.

Hypocrisy was the first internal threat to the church. Acts 5:1-11 gives the account of Ananias and Sapphira, a husband and a wife who thought they could lie to God and still be part of God's work in the church. God quickly and decisively judged their actions, demonstrating that He doesn't tolerate hypocrisy among His people. The church learned God's demand for holiness. Great respect for God came on the church (see v. 11).

Grumbling was the second internal threat to the church. As the church grew, its needs grew. Acts 6:1 reports that the apostles failed to meet the needs of the Hellenistic Jews in the fellowship, and people were grumbling. Grumbling sometimes means leaders have neglected to address a need adequately. Aubrey Malphurs advises:

> I would argue that often it's wise to listen to those who oppose your leadership, especially those who oppose it for the right reasons.[2]

The church didn't have enough leaders to oversee the daily distribution of food. The apostles' inability to serve all the members their daily rations resulted in division and grumbling.

Servants Are Appointed

Read Acts 6:1-6. What did the apostles suggest to address this need?

Verse 2:

Verse 3:

Verse 4:

As leaders, the apostles saw their role as ministers of the word of God. Their place in the church was to know, preach, and teach the words and deeds of Jesus, the Christ. That's what Jesus had commissioned them to do (see Matt. 28:19-20). Yet they were also responsible for the well-being of the fellowship. The church had members with an unmet need. To neglect it would mean division and hurt in the body. The apostles wisely shared the responsibility of this need with qualified members of the church, seven members who were "full of the Spirit and wisdom" (Acts 6:3). These seven were to "handle financial matters" (v. 2) for the neglected members so that the apostles could devote themselves "to prayer and to the preaching ministry" (v. 4). *Ministry* is the same word for *slave* that Jesus used when He said the great ones among His followers "must be a slave to all" (Mark 10:44). The apostles multiplied their leadership by delegating some of their responsibility and authority to others in order to meet needs in the fellowship.

SERVANT LEADERSHIP PRINCIPLE 6
Servant leaders share their responsibility and
authority with others to meet a greater need.

The currency of leadership includes power and authority. Through the use and sharing of these two leadership resources, leaders serve those in their care. This power isn't our own. Rather, …

> God has shared his power with us. We are stewards of the power that flows
> from God's blessing and from our connections to the heart and heartbeat
> of the community.[3]

Similarly, the authority isn't our own. That too comes from God, and because that's true, …

> The strongest and purest leaders do not need to rely on position or title.
> Their passion, wisdom, and authentic love carry all the authority that
> is needed.[4]

The apostles shared the responsibility of caring for others and delegated enough authority for the seven to make the necessary decisions to meet the people's needs.

Before ascending back to the Father, Jesus shared His authority with His disciples in order to meet the greater need of world evangelism:

> All authority has been given to Me in heaven
> and on earth. Go, therefore, and make disciples.
> **MATTHEW 28:18-19**

Jesus gave His followers authority before He gave them the responsibility of making disciples. Jesus shared His authority and responsibility with His disciples in order to spread the gospel around the world.

A Father-in-Law's Insight

The principles of delegation and empowerment aren't new. After the exodus Moses was responsible for leading the children of Israel to the promised land. One responsibility was to make decisions about disputes between people. The only problem was the great number of people! Moses sat from morning to evening settling arguments (see Ex. 18:13-16).

Read Exodus 18:17-18. What was Jethro's observation about the way Moses was leading the people?

Leaders wear out their followers and themselves when they try to lead alone. Too many church leaders suffer burnout because they think they're the only ones who can do the job. Owning responsibility for a task doesn't mean you alone can do it. Servant leaders know they're most effective when they trust others to work with them. Good leaders train and empower capable people to help them carry out their responsibilities.

Read Exodus 18:19-23. What was Jethro's suggestion to Moses to meet the people's needs and carry out his responsibility as a leader?

Verse 20:

Verse 21:

Verse 22:

Moses listened to his father-in-law. He taught the people and appointed judges over the nation. Moses delegated responsibility and authority to trustworthy judges to meet the needs of the people.

SERVANT LEADERSHIP PRINCIPLE 7
Servant leaders multiply their leadership by empowering others to lead.

Moses and Jesus' apostles met needs by sharing authority and responsibility with other leaders. Paul applied this same principle. He commanded Timothy to entrust what he'd taught the young church leader to "faithful men who will be able to teach others also" (2 Tim. 2:2).

Jesus multiplied His leadership by empowering His disciples with the Holy Spirit. He told His followers that they would "receive power when the Holy Spirit has come on you, and you will be My witnesses" (Acts 1:8). Empowerment always accompanies mission. Jesus gave His Holy Spirit to His disciples so that they would have power to witness about who He was and why the Father had sent Him. Jesus empowered His followers with the authority of His name and the power of His presence.

Results of Shared Leadership

Read Exodus 18:23. What did Jethro say would be the result if Moses did what he said?

In Acts 6:7 what happened when the apostles shared their leadership with the seven to care for members in the church?

The benefits of shared leadership include less stress on the leader and satisfied followers. The result is healthy growth and caring in the fellowship of the church. Shared leadership also results in more ministry and more focused leaders. Leaders serve by empowering others to lead with them.

Jesus followed these principles of servant leadership when He chose, trained, and sent the disciples out to build the kingdom of God. Matthew 10 records the way Jesus enlisted, trained, and sent out His disciples.

PERSONAL EVALUATION

If you're presently a leader in your church, choose the statement that best describes your honest feelings about leadership.

____ I'm tired and drained as a leader.

____ I feel as if I'm the only one who can do what I've been asked to do.

____ Enlisting and training others will take too much time, and my work will never get done.

____ I'm happy to delegate some of my responsibilities to others so that they can share in my joy of leadership.

____ I've been given much responsibility and little authority.

____ I've been trained as a leader and feel good about what I've been asked to do.

____ My church has enough trained leaders to help meet the needs of our fellowship.

What needs exist in your church and community that require good leadership?

Circle the needs you're responsible for in some way. List members you can enlist and train to help you meet this need.

End today's lesson by asking God to show you how He wants you to lead. Ask Him to show you others who can lead with you.

PRINCIPLES OF SERVANT LEADERSHIP

Principle 1: Servant leaders _____ themselves and wait for God to _____ them.

Principle 2: Servant leaders _____ Jesus rather than seek a _____.

Principle 3: Servant leaders give up personal _____ to find greatness in _____ to others.

Principle 4: Servant leaders can risk serving others because they _____ that God is in _____ of their lives.

Principle 5: Servant leaders take up Jesus' towel of _____ to meet the needs of _____.

Principle 6: Servant leaders share their _____ and _____ with others to meet a greater need.

Principle 7: Servant leaders _____ their leadership by _____ others to lead.

SUMMARY

- Servant leadership principle 6: Servant leaders share their responsibility and authority with others to meet a greater need.
- Servant leadership principle 7: Servant leaders multiply their leadership by empowering others to lead.
- Servant leaders know their value to the group and seek to stay focused on that role.
- The apostles enlisted others to help them meet needs in the body.
- Jethro helped Moses lead by suggesting that he share his leadership with capable men.
- God wants you to share your leadership with others so that they can experience the joy of servant leadership.

1. Stacy T. Rinehart, *Upside Down: The Paradox of Servant Leadership* (Colorado Springs: NavPress: 1998), 41.
2. Aubrey Malphurs, *Being Leaders: The Nature of Authentic Christian Leadership,* Kindle edition (Ada, MI: Baker Publishing Group, 2003), 126.
3. Robert E. Dale, *Seeds for the Future: Growing Organic Leaders for Living Churches* (Saint Louis: Lake Hickory Resources, 2005), 112.
4. Neil Cole, *Organic Leadership: Leading Naturally Right Where You Are,* Kindle edition (Ada, MI: Baker Books, 2009), 2140.

Day 5
YOU AS A SERVANT LEADER

True servant leadership embraces a humble sincerity that brings out the best in leaders and those they serve. That's exactly what Jesus did.[1]
KEN BLANCHARD

Today You Will
- Identify four elements of Jesus' leadership.
- Review the seven principles of servant leadership.
- Recall the events and teachings of Jesus' ministry that are the basis of each principle.
- Consider committing yourself to live like a servant leader in the weeks ahead.

Servant leadership isn't something you obtain. It isn't a position on the company chart you work toward. It isn't a career choice or a degree you earn. You don't gain it even after a six-week Bible study on the subject. Servant leadership grows from a relationship with the Master who came to serve rather than to be served. A servant's heart grows from time spent with Jesus and His teachings and from obeying what He said to do. He is your model of servant leadership and no book, course, or conference can substitute for your training time with the Master.

Four Key Elements of Jesus' Leadership

Jesus was a leader, and the focus of His leadership was empowering others to live out God's plan for their lives, not their own agendas. He served His disciples through a clear mission, direction, training, and a team of focused leaders to continue the mission of reconciliation after He returned to the Father.

When we observe Jesus' life, we see four key elements of His leadership.

1. Jesus had a clear mission. Jesus was a servant to the Father's mission for His life: to be the Suffering Servant Messiah (see Isa. 53:11), "to give His life—a ransom for many" (Mark 10:45). He didn't come to do His will "but the will of Him who sent Me" (John 6:38). Jesus humbled Himself and became a servant to God's mission for His life (see Phil. 2:6-8). The mission of God first belonged to Jesus.

The mission of God is everything for a servant leader who follows Jesus, answering the question "Why are we here?" The most familiar statement of this mission is what we call the Great Commission (see Matt. 28:19-20). As followers of Jesus go about their lives, we're to "make disciples" (v. 19) of Jesus. More specifically, God has commissioned with us the "ministry of reconciliation"(2 Cor. 5:18), in which we're "ambassadors for Christ" where we live, learn, work, and play (v. 20).

2. Jesus provided a clear direction. Jesus influenced His followers to leave their status quo and go where they wouldn't go on their own. The direction Jesus provided enabled His disciples to answer the question "Where are we going?" Jesus led them to trust "the kingdom of God has come near" and to "repent and believe in the good news" of His coming (Mark 1:15). He told vision stories in the form of parables to help them see God's preferred future for them. Jesus led those who trusted Him to the cross, where He suffered and died but was raised on the third day. Jesus kept the purposes and plans of God before His followers through His actions, teachings, and stories. Servant leaders like Jesus continually tell those they lead where they're going and what their lives are becoming through a loving relationship with Jesus Christ. This is the vision of a servant leader like Jesus.

3. Jesus trained His disciples to carry out the Father's mission. Jesus equipped them through His "Follow Me" method of training (Matt. 4:19) and trained them with the skills to be Kingdom people through His teaching and example. Equipping answers the question of those who join us on mission, "How do we do this?"

4. Jesus invested in a team of disciples. At the end of three years, when Jesus' time came to return to the Father, He commissioned His disciples to continue God's mission of reconciliation (see Matt. 28:19-20). To lead as a servant leader like Jesus is to invest in a core group of leaders who will carry on the mission in the leader's absence. Team leadership answers the question "Whom can we count on?"

Reviewing the Seven Principles of Servant Leadership

Today we want to review the seven principles of servant leadership. You'll record them and recall the events and teachings from Jesus' life that are the basis of each principle. When you've finished the review, you'll be asked to make a commitment to spend time with the Master, learning from Him how to live as a servant leader.

As you reflect on all you've experienced in this week's study, try to recall the seven principles and record them. If you need help, reread the foundational Scripture passage.

Principle 1: Based on Luke 14:7-11, servant leaders ...

Principle 2: Based on Mark 10:32-40, servant leaders ...

Principle 3: Based on Mark 10:41-45, servant leaders ...

Principle 4: Based on John 13:3, servant leaders ...

Principle 5: Based on John 13:4-11, servant leaders ...

Principle 6: Based on Acts 6:1-6, servant leaders ...

Principle 7: Based on Exodus 18:17-23, servant leaders ...

Choose to Be a Servant

Return to the seven principles you've just written. Circle principles that seem to be a part of your life today. Underline the biblical passages that have taught you the most about servant leadership. Be prepared to share your answers in your next group session.

You may be sensing now that this study was intended for someone other than yourself. You may feel that you aren't a leader in the church and that you'll never hold any position of leadership. On the other hand, you may now be a leader in the church, and this study has challenged everything you thought about leadership. In either case, you're still in the right place. Here's why.

Because you've trusted Christ to be your Savior and Lord, two things are true.

1. As a disciple of Jesus Christ, you're called to serve. Sometimes God calls you to lead others, but the pressure of leadership is off when you follow Jesus. Your priority becomes service. Any other model falls short of Jesus' example. Leadership in the body of Christ should always follow service. Meeting needs is your most important task as a servant leader.

2. You were created by God, bought with a price, called out for a purpose, and sent on mission. Success has already been achieved on the cross and in the resurrection of Christ. Your success is measured by your service. God created you for a purpose. He bought you with the price of His only Son's death (see 1 Cor. 6:20). God's only Son has commissioned you to make disciples (see Matt. 28:19-20) and to be an ambassador for Him:

> We are ambassadors for Christ, certain that God is appealing
> through us. We plead on Christ's behalf, "Be reconciled to God."
> **2 CORINTHIANS 5:20**

With those credentials, who needs the titles and headlines of leadership?

See, you belong here. God wants you to serve His people and those who need to know His love. This fact also applies to being a servant leader in your family as well as in ministries outside the church.

Jesus has called you to be a servant first and foremost. Leadership comes when the Host invites you to the head table for a season to guide and direct others. The training school for leaders in the body of Christ is with towel and washbasin in hand, kneeling at the feet of others.

PERSONAL EVALUATION

Prayerfully consider the following statements. Select those that represent your feelings at this time.

____ I never saw myself as a leader, but after this week of study, I believe God wants me to be a servant leader in my church.

____ I've been a leader in the church before, but this study has helped me see my role in a whole new way.

____ Jesus is the Lord of my life, and I commit myself to follow His examples and teachings of servant leadership.

____ I want to continue this discovery of servant leadership. I make a commitment now to spend time with the Master, to participate fully in the study, to learn to live as a servant leader, and to discover where Christ wants me to serve.

____ I'm uncertain about what all this means, but I'm willing to continue to seek God's will in my life.

____ I don't think I want to continue this study. These concepts are too foreign to me.

SUMMARY

- Servant leadership grows from a relationship with the Master who came to serve rather than to be served.
- When you follow Jesus, the pressure to lead is off. Your priority becomes service. Success has already been achieved on the cross and in the resurrection of Christ. Your success is measured by your service.
- God wants you to serve His people and those who need to know His love. This fact also applies to being a servant leader in your family as well as in ministries outside the church.

1. Ken Blanchard and Phil Hodges, *Lead like Jesus: Lessons from the Greatest Leadership Role Model of All Time,* Kindle edition (Nashville: Thomas Nelson, 2006), 213.

Week 2
LEADERS WHO SERVE, PART 1

This Week's Memory Verse

Based on the gift each one has received, use it to serve others, as good managers of the varied grace of God.
1 PETER 4:10

Ken Blanchard taught leadership as a full professor with tenure at the University of Massachusetts at age 35 and is best known for the globally popular book *The One-Minute Manager.* Through the witness of his close friend, Phil Hodges, he began to consider the things of God during the amazing success of that book. Other significant friends like Norman Vincent Peale, Bob Buford, and Bill Hybels shared their faith and guided him to Jesus. Blanchard testifies that after giving his life to the Lord in the late 1980s, he began to read the Bible, particularly the Gospels. As he studied, he became fascinated by the way Jesus led and transformed the lives of "twelve ordinary and unlikely people into the first generation of leaders of a movement that continues to affect the course of world history some two thousand years later." He then wrote:

> I soon became aware that everything I had ever taught or written about effective leadership during the past thirty-five years, Jesus did to perfection, beyond my ability to portray or describe.[1]

God had prepared Ken Blanchard to be His servant leader long before Ken would give his life to Him. When Ken made offered himself as a servant to God's call on his life, God led Ken and Phil to form the Lead like Jesus ministry. God has used those two servant leaders to share the message of servant leadership based on the role model of Jesus with millions worldwide.

This Week You Will

- Discover a biblical perspective on how God has prepared you to serve (day 1).
- Examine the biblical nature of the church and the purpose of spiritual gifts (day 2).
- Analyze the biblical pattern for setting gifted members aside for service and inventory your potential spiritual gifts (day 3).
- Better understand how God can use experiences in your life to prepare you to be a servant leader. You will record an important spiritual marker in your life (day 4).
- Learn how God works in people's lives to prepare them for servant leadership. You will examine your own life to see how God has used your experiences for His purposes (day 5).

Let's discover how God has prepared you for servant leadership.

God Prepares Servant Leaders to **SERVE**

SPIRITUAL GIFTS

EXPERIENCES

RELATIONAL STYLE

VOCATIONAL SKILLS

ENTHUSIASM

1. Ken Blanchard and Phil Hodges, *Lead like Jesus: Lessons from the Greatest Leadership Role Model of All Time*, Kindle edition (Nashville: Thomas Nelson, 2006), 10.

Day 1
GOD HAS PREPARED YOU TO SERVE

We tend to think we need leaders who serve,
but really we need servants who lead.[1]
NEIL COLE

Today You Will
- Learn how God wants you to use what He's given you.
- Examine the way Paul, the apostle, viewed his accomplishments.
- Recognize your achievements in light of biblical principles.
- Learn the meaning of SERVE.
- Take inventory of how God has molded you to be a servant leader.

Prepared for Service

Servant leaders know who they are in Christ Jesus. They know how God molded and gifted them for His use. They trust that God can use every experience to prepare them for ministry. Servant leaders don't need a place at a head table to give them confidence. They gladly serve in the kitchen, knowing that Christ is in control and they are where God has guided them. They trust that God has prepared them to serve for His glory, not their gain.

The world says you should use all you are for your own gain. Skill and gifts lead to success. Success leads to happiness, the self's highest achievement. God, on the other hand, says He's prepared you for His purposes to bring honor to Him:

Each of you should use whatever gift you have received to serve
others, as faithful stewards of God's grace in its various forms.
1 PETER 4:10, NIV

What does it mean to be a steward of God's grace?

The Bible says to use the spiritual gifts God gave you to serve others. You're to administer God's grace and gifts in your life "so that in all things God may be praised through Jesus Christ" (1 Pet. 4:11, NIV). The goal of all God's gifts is service to others.

The word *steward* describes a house servant who had charge over certain parts of his owner's assets. As a servant leader, you are a steward, or manager, of God's grace in your life. The apostle Paul understood his role in this way as well. Writing to the Christians in Ephesus, he told them of "the administration of God's grace" that God gave to him (Eph. 3:2). Paul's mission was to take the gospel to the Gentiles. He believed this mission was part of his stewardship of God's grace. Paul was a manager of God's grace for God's gain. Ralph Enlow Jr. enhances the meaning of *steward* this way:

> Stewards' significance is found not in terms of the domain *over which* they are sovereign but the Sovereign *under whom* they serve.[2]

Paul's Servant Outlook

Paul wrote that all he'd earned was in the loss column of his life's ledger sheet (see Phil. 3:7-8). All he had done and gained in worldly terms was worthless compared to knowing Christ. Let's take a moment to consider Paul's attitude about his accomplishments.

Suppose you were interviewing Paul for a ministry position in your church. Philippians 3:4-6 and 2 Corinthians 11:21-33 make up his résumé. Read both passages and list the items that impress you.

Philippians 3:4-6   **2 Corinthians 11:21-33**

You now come to the interview. You ask Paul to describe some of his experiences. You follow along from the pages of his letters. In the middle of the interview, he pauses and tells you he needs to explain something. He tells you what he wrote in Philippians 3:7-11.

Read Philippians 3:7-11. Record what you think his feelings would have been about what he'd done and who he was. How does that make you feel? Would you still hire him?

Paul considered everything he'd gained through his own achievement to be in the loss column of his life. The only profit item was knowing Christ.

Record some of your achievements below. Do you see them the same way Paul did, or do you put your confidence in them and consider them gain in your life? Indicate whether you consider your major achievements profits or losses in your life compared to knowing Christ.

My Major Achievements	Profit	Loss

Pause and pray. Ask God to help you see that all you are and have belongs to Him. Can you honestly state that nothing you've achieved or become is as valuable as knowing Christ? If not, begin to pray in earnest about your complete trust in Christ as your Savior and Lord.

Servant Leaders Are Leaders Who Serve

Let's use the acrostic SERVE as an outline for the way God has prepared you for His purposes. SERVE stands for:

Spiritual gifts—gifts God gives through His Holy Spirit to empower you for service
Experiences—events God allows that mold you into a servant leader
Relational style—behavioral traits God uses to give you a leadership style
Vocational skills—abilities you've gained through training and experience you can use to serve God
Enthusiasm—passion God has put in your heart for a particular ministry to others

In addition to your relationship with Christ, these five areas—spiritual gifts, experiences, relational style, vocational skills, and enthusiasm—become the raw materials God uses to mold you into a servant leader.

Paul was a servant leader. God uniquely prepared him to take the gospel of Jesus Christ to all people. Paul's submission to God's leadership and his stewardship of God's grace serve as models for how you can live your life for God. Look at what God did to prepare Paul for his life's mission.

Match each letter from the acrostic SERVE with the sentence that describes the way God prepared Paul for service.

____ 1. God gifted Paul as a prophet and teacher through His Holy Spirit.

____ 2. God used Paul's experiences as a Pharisee to help him understand the significance of Christ's death, burial, and resurrection. God used Paul's conversion experience and call to ministry to place him in a servant-leader role as a missionary.

____ 3. God gave Paul a strong relational style that aided him in the trials and setbacks that he experienced on mission.

____ 4. God gave Paul vocational skills to interpret Scripture so that he could share the good news. God also allowed Paul to learn how to make tents. This skill gave Paul the monetary means to carry out God's mission for his life.

____ 5. God ignited in Paul's heart a passion for people outside Israel to know that Jesus Christ is the Son of God.

God prepares leaders to serve His mission. God has prepared you to be a servant leader for His purposes. Answers: 1. S, 2. E, 3. R, 4. V, 5. E

Match the components of the SERVE acrostic with the appropriate statements:

____ 1. Gifts God gives through His Holy Spirit to empower you for service

____ 2. Behavioral traits God uses to give you a leadership style

____ 3. Passion God has put in your heart for a particular ministry to others

____ 4. Events God allows that mold you into a servant leader

____ 5. Abilities you've gained through training and experience you can use to serve God

The next two weeks of study will help you discover more about who you are in Christ and how God has already prepared you for servant leadership. Answers to matching: 1. S, 2. R, 3. E, 4. E, 5. V

SUMMARY

- God has prepared you for servant leadership.
- You're to use all God gives you to serve others.
- You're a steward of God's gracious gifts for His purposes.
- God has molded you to SERVE as a servant leader.

1. Neil Cole, *Organic Leadership: Leading Naturally Right Where You Are*, Kindle edition (Ada, MI: Baker Books, 2010), 2435.
2. Ralph E. Enlow Jr., *The Leader's Palette*, Kindle edition (Nashville: WestBow Press, 2013), 372.

Day 2
SPIRITUAL GIFTS, PART 1

Today You Will
- Examine the biblical nature of the church.
- Explore the purpose of spiritual gifts.
- Discover how every member has a place in the church.
- Define spiritual gifts.
- Review definitions of spiritual gifts.

God Prepares Servant Leaders to **SERVE**

☞ **SPIRITUAL GIFTS**

EXPERIENCES

RELATIONAL STYLE

VOCATIONAL SKILLS

ENTHUSIASM

Servant Leaders and Spiritual Gifts

Servant leaders know how God has gifted them for service in the body of Christ, the church. Servant leaders serve from their spiritual giftedness. Tenure and position don't count for servant leaders. They seek to lead from their God-given place in the body of Christ. The church works best when its members know how God has gifted them spiritually and when all members, empowered by their spiritual gifts, are in places of service.

Spiritual gifts are the key to understanding how God intends the church to function. They're part of God's gift of grace to believers (see Rom. 12:3-6; Eph. 4:7,11-13). Those who receive God's grace for salvation also receive God's gifts for service in Christ's body.

A spiritual gift is "a demonstration of the Spirit" (1 Cor. 12:7). It's not a special ability you develop on your own; that's a skill or a talent. You don't seek a spiritual gift. However, you should prayerfully seek to understand how God has already gifted you for His purposes.

God gives you spiritual gifts for a special purpose in the church when He graces you with salvation through Christ. Understanding spiritual gifts begins with knowing the biblical nature of the church.

The Church

Which drawing most clearly conveys the idea of church to you? Circle one.

   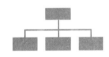

The Bible uses the analogy of a human body as the model for the church:

> As we have many parts in one body, and all the parts do not
> have the same function, in the same way we who are many are
> one body in Christ and individually members of one another.
> **ROMANS 12:4-5**

The body has many parts, but it's one. The body's many parts have different functions, but together they serve a single purpose. This analogy offers a different picture from the one many of today's churches follow.

Too many churches see themselves as institutions rather than living bodies. Too many churches see their members as servants of the organization rather than parts of a living body. Bodies grow and change. Institutions breed sameness. God chose the human body as the analogy of the church because the body of Christ is a living organism. The church is organized like a body, but what it does is more important than who's in what position on the organizational chart. The church grows through the power of the Holy Spirit. It functions best when all its members find their places of service in the mission of God as the church.

The Bible describes the church as the visible body of Christ:

> As the body is one and has many parts, and all the parts
> of that body, though many, are one body—so also is Christ.
> **1 CORINTHIANS 12:12**

The church is a living body, unified in purpose while diverse in its parts. Each member has a place in the body, and every part belongs. The church is many members gifted by God and united for service.

The Purpose of Spiritual Gifts

Read 1 Corinthians 12:7 and Ephesians 4:12.

> A demonstration of the Spirit is given to
> each person to produce what is beneficial.
> **1 CORINTHIANS 12:7**

> ... for the training of the saints in the work
> of ministry, to build up the body of Christ.
> **EPHESIANS 4:12**

Why did God give gifts to the church?

God gives spiritual gifts for the common good of the church. God gifts members of the church to equip and build up the body of Christ. He doesn't give us spiritual gifts for pride but for service. Servant leaders allow God's spiritual gifts to motivate them to serve.

Important to any study of spiritual gifts is God's work in the life of the believer and the church. You don't decide you want a certain gift and then go get it. God gives the gifts "as He wills" (1 Cor. 12:11). Spiritual gifts are part of God's design for a believer's life and for the life of the church. The Bible says:

> God has placed each one of the parts in one body just as He wanted.
> **1 CORINTHIANS 12:18**

Your goal as a servant leader is to discover how God in His grace has gifted you for service to His mission and to lead other believers in the same joy of discovering their spiritual gifts. These facts have implications for church leaders.

Choose the statement that represents the way you see your role as a church leader.

_____ I see myself as a leader who's responsible for managing an organization and finding people for service in our organizational chart.

_____ I see the church as a living organism put together by God for His purposes as part of His divine plan. My goal is to help people find where God is calling them to serve, not where I need them to work.

Everyone Belongs

The Bible uses the analogy of body parts to describe members of the church.

Read 1 Corinthians 12:14-20. In these verses what harmful thought did Paul address (see vv. 15-16)?

Some people feel that they don't belong in the church or that their participation doesn't matter because they aren't like others. In Corinth some Christians thought they didn't fit in because they didn't have the same gifts as others. Paul's response was:

> If the whole body were an eye, where would the hearing be? If the whole body were an ear, where would the sense of smell be? But now God has placed each one of the parts in one body just as He wanted.
> **1 CORINTHIANS 12:17-18**

Every member belongs to the body and has an important place in it. To feel you don't belong because you aren't like those who seem to be more visible is to deny the way God put the church together. Every member belongs.

Read 1 Corinthians 12:21-26. What feeling did Paul address in these verses (see v. 21)?

A member may feel he doesn't need others because he thinks his role is somehow more important. Churches divide when some members view others as less important than themselves. Someone in your church may think, *Preschool workers with the gift of service can't be as important as teachers with the gift of exhortation.* That thinking isn't biblical. Paul concluded that members who seem less important are actually given places of honor:

> God has put the body together, giving greater honor to the less
> honorable, so that there would be no division in the body
> **1 CORINTHIANS 12:24-25**

No member can say to another member, "I don't need you." God's purpose for bestowing a variety of gifts is to provide a variety of services as the church. Just as the body depends on the small thyroid gland for its health, every member depends on those in seemingly small places of service for the overall health of the church (see 1 Cor. 12:26).

What are some attitudes in your church that may cause members to feel they don't belong?

What ministries in your church may seem to be less important than the others, but in reality are essential to how the church carries out its mission?

The Spiritual Gifts

What comes to mind when you think of a spiritual gift?

For our study we'll use this definition of *spiritual gift*:

> A spiritual gift is an expression of the Holy Spirit in
> the lives of believers that empowers them to serve the
> mission of God as the body of Christ, the church.

Write your own definition of *spiritual gift*.

Romans 12:6-8; 1 Corinthians 12:8-10,28-30; Ephesians 4:11; and 1 Peter 4:9-11 contain representative lists of gifts and roles God has given to the church. Definitions of these gifts follow.[1]

LEADERSHIP. Leadership aids the body of Christ by leading and directing members to accomplish the goals and purposes of the church. Leadership motivates people to work together in unity toward common goals (see Rom. 12:8).

ADMINISTRATION/MANAGING. People with the gift of administration lead the body by steering others to remain on task. Administration enables the body to organize according to God-given purposes and long-term goals (see 1 Cor. 12:28).

TEACHING. Teaching is instructing members in the truths and doctrines of God's Word for the purposes of building up, unifying, and maturing the body (see Rom. 12:7; 1 Cor. 12:28; Eph. 4:11).

KNOWLEDGE. The gift of knowledge manifests itself in teaching and training in discipleship. It's the God-given ability to learn, know, and explain the precious truths of God's Word. A word of knowledge is a Spirit-revealed truth (see 1 Cor. 12:8).

WISDOM. Wisdom is the gift that discerns the work of the Holy Spirit in the body and applies His teachings and actions to the needs of the body (see 1 Cor. 12:8).

PROPHECY. The gift of prophecy is boldly proclaiming the Word of God. This builds up the body and leads to conviction of sin. Prophecy manifests itself in preaching and teaching (see Rom. 12:6; 1 Cor. 12:10; Eph. 4:11).

DISCERNMENT/DISTINGUISHING BETWEEN SPIRITS. Discernment aids the body by recognizing the true intentions of those within or related to the body. Discernment tests the message and actions of others for the protection and well-being of the body (see 1 Cor. 12:10).

EXHORTATION. Possessors of this gift encourage members to be involved in and enthusiastic about the work of the Lord. Members with this gift are good counselors and motivate others to service. Exhortation exhibits itself in preaching, teaching, and ministry (see Rom. 12:8).

SHEPHERDING/PASTORING. The gift of shepherding is manifested in people who look out for the spiritual welfare of others. Although pastors, like shepherds, care for members of the church, this gift isn't limited to a pastor or staff member (see Eph. 4:11).

FAITH. Faith trusts God to work beyond human capabilities. Believers with this gift encourage others to trust in God in the face of apparently insurmountable odds (see 1 Cor. 12:9).

EVANGELISM. God gifts his church with evangelists to lead others to Christ effectively and enthusiastically. This gift builds up the body by adding new members to its fellowship (see Eph. 4:11).

APOSTLESHIP. The church sends apostles from the body to plant churches or be missionaries. Apostles motivate the body to look beyond its walls in order to carry out the Great Commission (see 1 Cor. 12:28; Eph. 4:11).

SERVICE/HELPS. People with the gift of service/helps recognize practical needs in the body and joyfully give assistance to meeting those needs. Christians with this gift don't mind working behind the scenes (see Rom. 12:7; 1 Cor. 12:28; 1 Pet. 4:10-11).

MERCY. Cheerful acts of compassion characterize people with the gift of mercy. People with this gift aid the body by empathizing with hurting members. They keep the body healthy and unified by keeping others aware of needs in the church (see Rom. 12:8).

GIVING. Members with the gift of giving give freely and joyfully to the work and mission of the body. Cheerfulness and liberality are characteristics of individuals with this gift (see Rom. 12:8).

HOSPITALITY. People with this gift have the ability to make visitors, guests, and strangers feel at ease. They often use their homes to entertain guests. People with this gift integrate new members into the body of Christ (see 1 Pet. 4:9).

God has gifted you with an expression of His Holy Spirit to support His worldwide vision and mission for the church: to reach all people with the gospel of Christ. God wants you, as a servant leader, to know the ways He's gifted you. This knowledge enables you to identify where He wants you to serve as part of His vision and mission for the church.

Tomorrow you'll learn more about spiritual gifts and discover the gifts God may have graced you with for service in His body.

SUMMARY

- Servant leaders know how God has gifted them for service.
- Those who receive God's grace for salvation also receive God's gifts for service in Christ's body.
- The church is a living body, unified in purpose while diverse in its parts.
- Every member belongs to the body.
- God gives spiritual gifts for the common good of the church.
- A spiritual gift is an expression of the Holy Spirit in the lives of believers that empowers them to serve the mission of God as the body of Christ, the church.
- God wants you, as a servant leader, to know the ways He's gifted you.

1. These definitions exclude the sign gifts because of some confusion that accompanies these gifts and because they're difficult to fit into ministries in many churches' ministry base.

Day 3
SPIRITUAL GIFTS, PART 2

Today You Will
- Examine how God sets aside members for service in the church.
- Read about one church's effort to empower its people for ministry.
- Study each of the spiritual gifts.
- Discover ways God has gifted you for service.

Spiritual gifts are God's way of empowering members of Christ's body for ministry. They form the basis of how churches should structure their ministries. Traditionally, church leaders build an organizational chart showing leadership needs and then seek to fill those needs with people. In contrast, servant-led churches seek to build their organizational chart after they learn how God has assembled the church. Church structure should be open to include ministries that may not usually be part of that church's local ministry. Churches must move from a position where people serve the structure of the church to a place where its structure serves people's needs. Servant leaders lead by serving the church, empowered by the Spirit's gifts in their lives.

How God Sets Members Aside for Service

Acts 13 begins, "In the church that was at Antioch there were prophets and teachers."

> **Read Acts 13:1-3. What did the church do with two of the men who were recognized as prophets and teachers?**

Under the leadership of the Holy Spirit, the church in Antioch set aside Barnabas and Saul, whom they saw as spiritually gifted "prophets and teachers" (v. 1).[1] Recognizing God's gift in their lives, the church then followed God's Spirit to set them aside for service. This is the church's pattern for setting aside members for service.

Write the verse number from Acts 13:1-3 beside the corresponding action.

____ **The church body observed spiritual giftedness in members' lives.**
____ **The church obeyed God's call and commissioned two people
to be on mission with God.**
____ **During worship and prayer God called the church to set people
aside for service.**

Let's look first at how the Antioch church observed these gifts in Saul's and Barnabas's lives. Saul and Barnabas were among a group of members in the Antioch church recognized as having the gifts of teaching and prophecy (see v. 1).

Luke, the writer of Acts, noted that Barnabas and Saul "met with the church and taught large numbers" (11:26). The church observed and took note of ways members served other members. Later, on the first missionary journey, we learn that Paul possessed the gift of prophecy from the fact that the Lycaonians thought he was the god Hermes "because he was the main speaker" (14:12).

How did the church know to set these men apart? The Bible states that while they were "ministering to the Lord and fasting," the Holy Spirit told the church to set apart Barnabas and Saul "for the work I have called them to" (13:2). When the church worships and seeks God's will, God reveals His plans for different members in the church.

What did the church do to acknowledge God's call and their members' gifts? After the church "had fasted, prayed, and laid hands on them, they sent them off" (v. 3). The church was obedient to God's call by praying and fasting to know His will. They placed their hands on Saul and Barnabas as a sign of God's call in their lives and sent them off. The church set its members aside for God's service and encouraged them to do that service.

Based on what you just studied, describe your understanding of God's plan for knowing and setting apart members for service.

Evaluate your church's process for setting members aside for service. Circle the number closest to the statement that represents your church.

1	2	3	4	5
Nothing like the Antioch church			**Like the Antioch church**	

One Church's Story

I sensed God was calling our church to empower people for service through the discovery of spiritual gifts. I put together a task force of our best teachers to find the tools to inventory the gifts and to develop a strong foundation of the biblical teaching on spiritual gifts. We met, studied, and prayed for several weeks. We came together with one mind concerning what the Bible teaches about spiritual gifts and their purpose in the church. We decided on an inventory and a plan to teach the church about the gifts.

We took a month of Sundays to lead our members in the study and discovery of spiritual gifts. I preached on one aspect of the gifts each Sunday. The task-force members then taught the same topic the next week in adult Bible-study classes. At the end of the four weeks, we invited every member to complete a spiritual-gifts inventory and turn in the results the following week. This was the beginning of our membership profiles, which listed the spiritual gifts of each member. This information helped our membership-involvement team match members with ministry. Spiritual-gift discovery was part of our membership workshop and our ongoing "Finding Your Place of Ministry" seminar that we offered once a quarter. This *Jesus on Leadership* Bible study could be used the same way.

Never before that month-long emphasis had so many people stepped forward to find a place of service in the church, and never had many new ministries begun in such a short period of time. As members discovered how God had gifted them for service, they felt free to pursue that ministry with joy and certainty.[2]

What activities has your church undertaken to help members discover their spiritual gifts and find a place of ministry? Choose an activity you've done or are considering in your church.

_____ **Your church's leaders make spiritual gifts the basis of ministry in the body.**

_____ **Your church has studied the biblical basis for spiritual gifts.**

_____ **Your church has held an emphasis on spiritual gifts.**

_____ **Your church has a way to empower members for ministry through the discovery of spiritual gifts.**

_____ **Your church provides ongoing training of new and current members about spiritual gifts.**

YOUR SPIRITUAL GIFTS

God has gifted you for service in Christ's body, the church (see 1 Cor. 12:7). His goal is for you to prepare others for service in the church (see Eph. 4:12). As a servant leader, you're to use your spiritual gifts for the common good of the body. God gifted you for His glory, not your gain. God gifted you to build up His church, not your ego.

> You're about to complete one of the most important activities in this workbook. As you do so, find a quiet place where you can relax, forget the problems of the world for a while, and spend time thinking and praying about the special gifts God has given you. Complete the spiritual-gifts survey that follows.[3] Remember that spiritual gifts are for serving others and meeting needs as part of the church's mission. Every gift empowers members to minister through the body of Christ.

Spiritual-Gifts Survey

DIRECTIONS

This isn't a test, so there are no wrong answers. The spiritual-gifts survey consists of 80 statements. Some items reflect concrete actions, other items are descriptive traits, and still others are statements of belief.

Select the one response you feel best characterizes yourself and place that number in the blank provided. Record your answer in the blank beside each item.

Don't spend too much time on any one item. Remember, it isn't a test. Usually, your immediate response is best.

Give an answer for each item. Don't skip any items. Don't ask others how they're answering or how they think you should answer. Work at your own pace.

Your response choices are:
5   Highly characteristic of me/definitely true for me
4   Most of the time this would describe me/be true for me.
3   Frequently characteristic of me/true for me—about 50 percent of the time
2   Occasionally characteristic of me/true for me—about 25 percent of the time
1   Not at all characteristic of me/definitely untrue for me

_____ 1. I have the ability to organize ideas, resources, time, and people effectively.
_____ 2. I am willing to study and prepare for the task of teaching.
_____ 3. I am able to relate the truths of God to specific situations.
_____ 4. I have a God-given ability to help others grow in their faith.
_____ 5. I possess a special ability to communicate the truth of salvation.
_____ 6. I have the ability to make critical decisions when necessary.
_____ 7. I am sensitive to the hurts of people.
_____ 8. I experience joy in meeting needs through sharing possessions.
_____ 9. I enjoy studying.
_____ 10. I have delivered God's message of warning and judgment.
_____ 11. I am able to sense the true motivation of persons and movements.
_____ 12. I have a special ability to trust God in difficult situations.
_____ 13. I have a strong desire to contribute to the establishment of new churches.
_____ 14. I take action to meet physical and practical needs rather than merely talking about or planning to help.
_____ 15. I enjoy entertaining guests in my home.
_____ 16. I can adapt my guidance to fit the maturity of those working with me.
_____ 17. I can delegate and assign meaningful work.

_____ 18. I have an ability and desire to teach.

_____ 19. I am usually able to analyze a situation correctly.

_____ 20. I have a natural tendency to encourage others.

_____ 21. I am willing to take the initiative in helping other Christians grow in their faith.

_____ 22. I have an acute awareness of the emotions of other people, such as loneliness, pain, fear, and anger.

_____ 23. I am a cheerful giver.

_____ 24. I spend time digging into facts.

_____ 25. I feel that I have a message from God to deliver to others.

_____ 26. I can recognize when a person is genuine/honest.

_____ 27. I am a person of vision (a clear mental portrait of a preferable future given by God). I am able to communicate vision in such a way that others commit to making the vision a reality.

_____ 28. I am willing to yield to God's will rather than question and waver.

_____ 29. I would like to be more active in getting the gospel to people in other lands.

_____ 30. It makes me happy to do things for people in need.

_____ 31. I am successful in getting a group to do its work joyfully.

_____ 32. I am able to make strangers feel at ease.

_____ 33. I have the ability to plan learning approaches.

_____ 34. I can identify those who need encouragement.

_____ 35. I have trained Christians to be more obedient disciples of Christ.

_____ 36. I am willing to do whatever it takes to see others come to Christ.

_____ 37. I am attracted to people who are hurting.

_____ 38. I am a generous giver.

_____ 39. I am able to discover new truths.

_____ 40. I have spiritual insights from Scripture concerning issues and people that compel me to speak out.

_____ 41. I can sense when a person is acting in accord with God's will.

_____ 42. I can trust in God even when things look dark.

_____ 43. I can determine where God wants a group to go and help it get there.

_____ 44. I have a strong desire to take the gospel to places where it has never been heard.

_____ 45. I enjoy reaching out to new people in my church and community.

_____ 46. I am sensitive to the needs of people.

_____ 47. I have been able to make effective and efficient plans for accomplishing the goals of a group.

_____ 48. I often am consulted when fellow Christians are struggling to make difficult decisions.

_____ 49. I think about how I can comfort and encourage others in my congregation.

_____ 50. I am able to give spiritual direction to others.

_____ 51. I am able to present the gospel to lost persons in such a way that they accept the Lord and His salvation.

_____ 52. I possess an unusual capacity to understand the feelings of those in distress.

_____ 53. I have a strong sense of stewardship based on the recognition that God owns all things.

_____ 54. I have delivered to other persons messages that have come directly from God.

_____ 55. I can sense when a person is acting under God's leadership.

_____ 56. I try to be in God's will continually and be available for His use.

_____ 57. I feel that I should take the gospel to people who have different beliefs from me.

_____ 58. I have an acute awareness of the physical needs of others.

_____ 59. I am skilled in setting forth positive and precise steps of action.

_____ 60. I like to meet visitors at church and make them feel welcome.

_____ 61. I explain Scripture in such a way that others understand it.

_____ 62. I can usually see spiritual solutions to problems.

_____ 63. I welcome opportunities to help people who need comfort, consolation, encouragement, and counseling.

_____ 64. I feel at ease in sharing Christ with nonbelievers.

_____ 65. I can influence others to perform to their highest God-given potential.

_____ 66. I recognize the signs of stress and distress in others.

_____ 67. I desire to give generously and unpretentiously to worthwhile projects and ministries.

_____ 68. I can organize facts into meaningful relationships.

_____ 69. God gives me messages to deliver to His people.

_____ 70. I am able to sense whether people are being honest when they tell of their religious experiences.

_____ 71. I enjoy presenting the gospel to persons of other cultures and backgrounds.

_____ 72. I enjoy doing little things that help people.

_____ 73. I can give a clear, uncomplicated presentation.

_____ 74. I have been able to apply biblical truth to the specific needs of my church.

_____ 75. God has used me to encourage others to live Christlike lives.

_____ 76. I have sensed the need to help other people become more effective in their ministries.

_____ 77. I like to talk about Jesus to those who do not know Him.

_____ 78. I have the ability to make strangers feel comfortable in my home.

_____ 79. I have a wide range of study resources and know how to secure information.

_____ 80. I feel assured that a situation will change for the glory of God even when the situation seem impossible.

SCORING YOUR SURVEY

Follow these directions to figure your score for each spiritual gift.

1. Place in each box your numerical response (1–5) to the item number indicated below the box.
2. For each gift, add the numbers in the boxes and record the total in the TOTAL box.

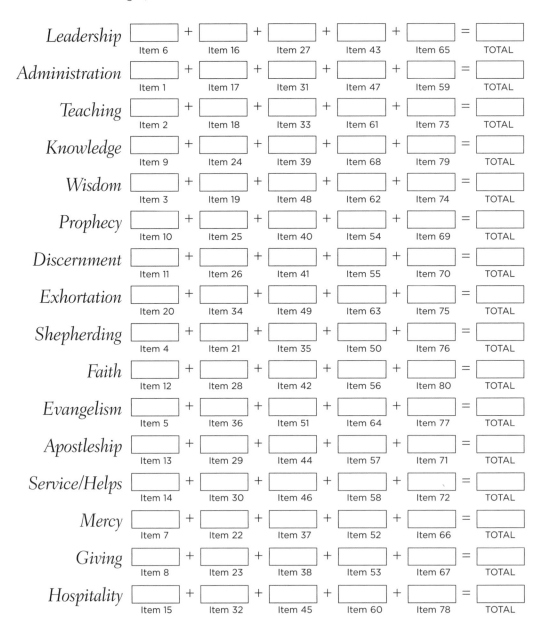

Leadership Item 6	+ Item 16	+ Item 27	+ Item 43	+ Item 65	= TOTAL
Administration Item 1	+ Item 17	+ Item 31	+ Item 47	+ Item 59	= TOTAL
Teaching Item 2	+ Item 18	+ Item 33	+ Item 61	+ Item 73	= TOTAL
Knowledge Item 9	+ Item 24	+ Item 39	+ Item 68	+ Item 79	= TOTAL
Wisdom Item 3	+ Item 19	+ Item 48	+ Item 62	+ Item 74	= TOTAL
Prophecy Item 10	+ Item 25	+ Item 40	+ Item 54	+ Item 69	= TOTAL
Discernment Item 11	+ Item 26	+ Item 41	+ Item 55	+ Item 70	= TOTAL
Exhortation Item 20	+ Item 34	+ Item 49	+ Item 63	+ Item 75	= TOTAL
Shepherding Item 4	+ Item 21	+ Item 35	+ Item 50	+ Item 76	= TOTAL
Faith Item 12	+ Item 28	+ Item 42	+ Item 56	+ Item 80	= TOTAL
Evangelism Item 5	+ Item 36	+ Item 51	+ Item 64	+ Item 77	= TOTAL
Apostleship Item 13	+ Item 29	+ Item 44	+ Item 57	+ Item 71	= TOTAL
Service/Helps Item 14	+ Item 30	+ Item 46	+ Item 58	+ Item 72	= TOTAL
Mercy Item 7	+ Item 22	+ Item 37	+ Item 52	+ Item 66	= TOTAL
Giving Item 8	+ Item 23	+ Item 38	+ Item 53	+ Item 67	= TOTAL
Hospitality Item 15	+ Item 32	+ Item 45	+ Item 60	+ Item 78	= TOTAL

GRAPHING YOUR PROFILE

1. For each gift, place a mark across the bar at the point that corresponds to your TOTAL for that gift.
2. For each gift, shade the bar below the mark you've drawn.
3. The resultant graph provides a picture of your gifts. Gifts for which the bars are tall are the ones in which you appear to be strongest. Gifts for which the bars are very short are the ones in which you appear not to be strong. For a definition of each gift, see day 1 of this week's study.

SCORE

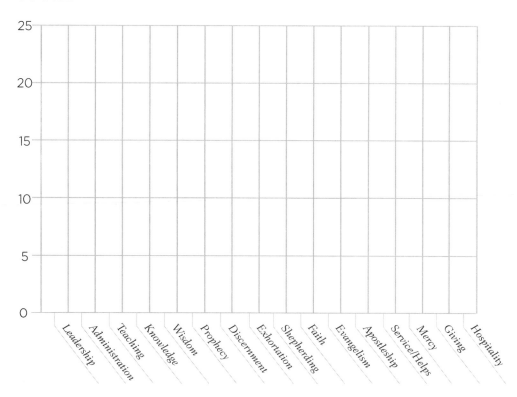

Now that you've completed the survey, answer the following questions.

The gifts I've begun to discover in my life are:

____ **After prayer and worship I'm beginning to sense that God wants me to use my spiritual gifts to serve Christ's body by ...**

____ **I'm not yet sure how God wants me to use my gifts to serve others. But I'm committed to prayer and worship, seeking wisdom and opportunities to use the gifts I've received from God.**

End today's study by asking God to help you know how He's gifted you for service and how you can begin to use this gift in ministry to others. This survey is only a starting point in discovering the Holy Spirit's gifts in your life. To confirm what you've begun to learn through this survey, continue to study the Bible on the topic, praying often for God to guide you; rely on the input of those who know you well to affirm what you believe are your gifts; and begin serving in ministry.

SUMMARY

- Spiritual gifts are God's way of empowering members of Christ's body for ministry.
- God has given you a spiritual gift to empower you for ministry to others.
- The church can function according to the biblical pattern revealed in the Antioch church by observing and recognizing the spiritual gifts of its members, hearing God's call to set members aside for service, setting members aside for their place of service, and empowering them to perform that ministry.
- God gifted you for His glory, not your gain.

1. You can interpret "prophets and teachers" (Acts 13:1) as either spiritual gifts or roles in the church. For example, the Bible describes teaching as a gift in Romans 12:7 and as a role in Ephesians 4:11. The Bible lists prophecy the same two ways. The early church didn't equate gifts with positions in the church. A prophet didn't have the paid position of preacher; rather, he served the church by proclaiming God's good news in Christ. See 1 Corinthians 14 to get a definition of the gift of prophecy compared to the gift of speaking in tongues.
2. Along with this emphasis on spiritual gifts, we retooled our church's organization to allow members to begin new ministries, and we gave them authority and resources to perform those ministries.
3. This survey excludes the sign gifts because of some confusion that accompanies these gifts and because they're difficult to fit into ministries in many churches' ministry base.

Day 4
EXPERIENCES, PART 1

Jesus was not spared the heart-shaping work that God intends for all his leaders. From eternity past, the heart of the Son was molded for his mission. From the moment of miraculous conception to his ascension, every detail of his earthly life was superintended in order to fashion the heart of the Father in him.[1]

REGGIE MCNEAL

Today You Will

- See ways God works in history to accomplish His will.
- Learn how Paul saw his life before and after his conversion.
- Become aware of how God uses experiences to accomplish His will.
- Record an important spiritual marker in your life.

God Prepares Servant Leaders to SERVE

SPIRITUAL GIFTS

☛ ### EXPERIENCES

RELATIONAL STYLE

VOCATIONAL SKILLS

ENTHUSIASM

The God of History

God is the God of history. History is where God carries out His plans. But God isn't just the God of then and there. He's the God of here and now. As the Creator, God is sovereign over all events of history. Events happen as God either allows them or ordains them to take place. History is what Jesus Christ's becoming human was all about. God entered history to save creation from the penalty of its sin against Him. The word *incarnation*, which comes from a Latin term, means *in flesh*. In Jesus Christ, God came in flesh. The Gospel according to John states that:

> The Word became flesh
> and took up residence among us.
> **JOHN 1:14**

God has always worked in history—His story—to carry out His purposes.

Servant leaders trust that God also works in their personal histories to bring about His plan for their lives. Experiences become God's crucible to mold you into His image. Servant leaders are confident that events that happen to them and around them are part of God's sovereign work in creation.

God and Paul's Experiences

Look at Paul's (Saul's) life. You read his résumé in day 1. Now let's take inventory of his life experiences.

Answer the questions as you examine the following Scripture passages.

Where did Saul grow up (see Acts 21:39)?

What were his nationality and citizenship (see Acts 22:3,25-29)?

Where was he educated, and who was his teacher (see Acts 21:17; 22:3)?

Before his conversion what did he do to try to stop the heresy of the Christ cult (see Acts 22:4-5; 1 Cor. 15:9)?

Whose death did Saul witness and give his approval (see Acts 7:54–8:1)?

Up to that point how would you describe God's work in Saul's life?

Here are some ways God prepared Saul of Tarsus for his unique role to carry the gospel around the world to all ethnic groups through his life experiences.

- Paul was born a Jew, and he had the rights and privileges of a Roman citizen.
- As a Jew, he knew God's covenant relationship with Israel. He'd learned the history of God's work with His people. He knew and trusted the God of Abraham, Isaac, and Jacob.
- As a Roman citizen, he had the legal and cultural advantages that position offered. Paul had the best education the Jewish people could offer.
- He studied under one of the leading Jewish teachers of his day. He learned the Scriptures of the Old Testament and how to interpret them and apply them to life.
- He developed the skill of working with leather and making tents, which provided financial support and a network of marketplace associates.
- Because he was multilingual, he was able to communicate with many ethnic groups.

Although Saul didn't call Jesus the Messiah, the Son of God early in his life, God used all his life experiences as a foundation for what He would do later in the apostle's life.

When Saul heard the followers of Jesus calling this man the Messiah, he began to attack them. His temperament drove him to excel toward his goal as a leader among the people of Israel. Saul persecuted the church with zeal and conviction. However, God took all of Saul's positive and negative experiences and used them for His glory. God transformed Saul's zeal to destroy the church into a passion to build it through an encounter with the risen Lord. That's the difference God makes in a person's life.

God and Your Experiences

God can take what's already happened in your life to help accomplish His will. He can mold you into a tool of His grace. He can break into your life to make you a new creation for His purposes.

Paul considered his experience on the road to Damascus the turning point of his life. Each time he told his story, he included that spiritual turning point.

Read Paul's testimony in Acts 22:3-21. Summarize the events in his life that he included in his witness.

His life before he met Jesus (see vv. 3-5):

His experience of conversion and call (see vv. 6-16):

His life since his encounter with Christ (see vv. 17-21):

Henry Blackaby calls events like Paul's conversion "spiritual markers."[2] Blackaby says a spiritual marker "identifies a time of transition, decision, or direction when I clearly know God has guided me."[3] Spiritual markers remind you that God is at work in your history. Remembering them helps you recognize God's work in your life and ways He's unfolding His plan for your life.

Read the following passages and identify the spiritual markers in Simon Peter's life.

Peter's Spiritual Markers

Mark 1:16-18

Mark 8:27-30

Mark 14:66-72

John 21:15-22

Acts 2:1-13

Acts 10:9-38

God defined His will for Paul and Peter as they encountered God in history. He will do the same in your life.

A Personal Marker

The summer before my senior year in high school, I went with my youth group on a mission trip. We went to a Navajo Indian reservation in New Mexico to lead Vacation Bible Schools and do construction work in churches. It was everything a mission trip was supposed to be. There were no indoor bathrooms, so we drove into town one day to bathe in the local school gym. I rode with my team for an hour across open desert to get to the village where we held our Vacation Bible School. I remember sharing my faith with a Navajo Indian boy, who accepted Christ as his Savior.

On Thursday evening that week, before the revival services we held under a tent, I walked out into the open desert. Lightning and thunder exploded over the mesas surrounding the compound where we'd pitched our tent. I felt the presence of God, and I sensed Him ask me a simple question: "What do you enjoy doing?" I replied, "This. Being with Christian people doing Your work." God said, "Then go do that." I did. When we got home and shared our experiences that Sunday evening in church, I went forward to offer my life to the full-time service of God. I changed my plans to attend a state college. Instead, I enrolled in a Baptist university and began my training as a minister of the gospel.

That spiritual marker has shaped my life. It helped me decide what college to attend, what major to choose, and the path my life should take. Even as I write this, I recall the deep certainty that comes from knowing God has a special plan for my life. He cared enough to break into history to reveal that plan to me.

Your Spiritual Markers

You have similar events in your life when God has made His will clear to you, when He broke into history, and you know He spoke to you. He may have confirmed a decision you'd made. He may have revealed something new about who He is. Take a moment to describe some of your most important encounters with God. Write as if you're telling a friend about these life-changing moments. Start with your salvation experience. Don't worry if you don't have a dramatic desert story. God works in everyday events to shape you into His likeness. Spiritual markers can be anything from a burning bush to a child's gentle touch.

My Spiritual Markers: Events That Changed My Life

If you don't have a life-changing encounter with Christ to write about, consider your relationship with Jesus. Pause and ask God to confirm His presence in your life. If you know you haven't trusted Christ as your Savior and Lord, be assured that if you'll confess your sins and call on the name of Jesus, you'll be saved (see Rom. 10:9-10). Talk with your group leader, a pastor, or a respected Christian friend.

SUMMARY

- Events happen as God either allows or ordains them to take place.
- Servant leaders trust that God works in their personal history to bring about His plan in their lives.
- God used the experiences in Saul's life to prepare him for his work as an ambassador of the gospel.
- God allowed several spiritual markers in Peter's life to confirm His will for the fisherman.
- An encounter with Christ can transform every personal experience for the glory of God.

1. Reggie McNeal. *A Work of Heart: Understanding How God Shapes Spiritual Leaders,* Kindle edition (Hoboken, NJ: Jossey-Bass, 2009), 1095.
2. Henry Blackaby, Richard Blackaby, and Claude King, *Experiencing God: Knowing and Doing the Will of God* (Nashville: LifeWay, 2007), 123.
3. Ibid., 126.

Day 5
EXPERIENCES, PART 2

Today You Will

- Learn how God has worked in other people's lives to accomplish His will.
- Examine Esther's life to identify ways God guided her life for His purposes.
- Use a timeline to mark your experiences with God.
- Evaluate your life to identify ways God has used your personal experiences.

Patsy's Story

Patsy's parents were deaf. But Patsy could hear, and she learned how to live in the worlds of both the hearing and the deaf. When Patsy became an adult and a mother herself, she wanted to work with teenagers. Patsy and her husband decided to move their church membership to a church closer to home so that their teenage daughter could be with friends who went to school with her.

One Sunday a deaf couple asked Patsy to interpret a worship service for them. She reluctantly did so. Another deaf couple learned that Patsy interpreted for worship services, and they asked Patsy to interpret for them. She agreed to do so once a month. Soon a small group of deaf families gathered for Bible study and worship. Patsy began to meet with and minister to the group regularly. A vital deaf fellowship developed in the church.

Patsy didn't choose to be the child of deaf parents. At times she thought she was unlucky to have parents who couldn't hear, and she wasn't necessarily proud that she knew a second language. However, she allowed God to work in her life to bring about His plan for her and others. Because Patsy was faithful to God's leadership in her life, she soon led a vital ministry to deaf individuals and families that continues to this day. Patsy is a servant leader. She served the needs of those who asked for her help and soon found herself leading. She accepted the experiences in her life as God's design for His purposes.

Servant leaders accept experiences in their lives as the raw material of God's work as He shapes who they are.

Identify any feelings you felt in common with Patsy as you read her story.

Let's look at another person God put in a special place to accomplish His purposes.

Esther's Story

Esther, the cousin of an obscure Jew, was in exile in Persia, a stranger in a foreign land. God, however, made her beautiful. Her cousin, Mordecai, heard about a beauty pageant for the king. The Persian emperor didn't like his wife's stubborn attitude, and he had taken his advisers' counsel to choose a new wife from all the women of the land. God allowed Esther to find favor with the king, and he chose her for his wife.

The climax of the story came when the king allowed Haman, a member of the his staff, to decree the death of all Jews. Haman wanted Mordecai dead because the Jew wouldn't bow down to him. So Haman decided to exterminate all the Jews. Mordecai learned of Haman's plan and told his cousin, the queen. He insisted that she intercede for her people, and Esther insisted she could be killed in the process. Mordecai reminded her that if the law stood, she would die anyway. He also let her know that maybe God allowed her to become the queen "for such a time as this" (Esth. 4:14). Esther asked Mordecai and her fellow citizens to pray for her.

Esther trusted God. She approached the king and requested that he attend a banquet along with Haman. At the meal she told the king she was a Jew and that a new law would allow her death. The king went ballistic! He asked who would make such a law that would kill the queen. Esther pointed to Haman. When the king saw Haman pleading with Esther, he thought Haman was attacking her. He executed Haman on the same gallows that Haman had prepared for Mordecai. Esther encouraged the king to write a law that allowed the Jews to protect themselves on the day they were to be killed. Jews still celebrate Purim, the day God allowed them to protect themselves and survive the exile.

Esther's story shows how God uses experiences in a person's life to bring about His ultimate plans. God permitted certain events God in Esther's life and used them to accomplish His will.

As you read the following passages, list the experience and the way God used each one.

Experience	How God Used It
Esther 2:5-7	
Esther 2:8	
Esther 2:17	

Esther 4:14

Esther 5:7-8

Esther 7:1-10

Esther 8:8,11

God used events in the lives of Esther and Patsy to accomplish a bigger plan in history. He can do the same in your life.

Your Life Map

Your life experiences form a map of God's work in your life. God uses every moment—from your birth and family of origin to the events of today—to mold you into a servant leader for His purposes. You can have hope for the future when you recognize God's powerful presence and purposeful activity in your past.

Creating a map of your life experiences provides an opportunity to examine significant events and patterns in your life in order to recognize the many ways God has been at work that you might not have realized before. The goal is to make a visual representation of the way God has molded you into the likeness of His Son through the events of your life, no matter how painful or exciting they may have been.

Create a timeline of your life by recording the major events from your story on a line that represents years. Mark your birth and the spiritual markers you wrote about in day 4.

How has God used the events on your timeline to make you the potential servant leader you can be today?

My Spiritual Markers   **How God Used These Events**

Moving Toward Your Destination

One of my favorite stories is *The Horse and His Boy* by C. S. Lewis. In the story an orphan named Shasta meets a speaking horse from Narnia. They agree to travel together. A creature pursues them throughout their trip home. Events happen that frighten Shasta, and he wonders why so many bad things keep happening to him. Shasta declares himself "the most unfortunate boy that ever lived in the whole world."[1] Finally, Shasta and the creature meet. The animal that pursued Shasta and his horse turns out to be Aslan, the lion and God figure in the book. Aslan describes each event that Shasta thought was bad and dangerous. Every event had guided Shasta to make his way to Narnia. Aslan tells Shasta his story and about his home in Narnia. When the boy and his horse arrive in Narnia, he discovers that he's a prince and heir to the throne. Looking back, Shasta sees that Aslan guided him through difficult experiences to receive his true inheritance.

I love this story because it paints a picture of providence. God uses good and bad events in our lives to guide us to our inheritance in Christ Jesus. God is at work in the circumstances and happenings of your life, and He's been at work throughout your whole life. He's been guiding each of us to our inheritance as children of God. God can use any event in our lives to guide us to His kingdom. As you prayerfully consider how God has worked in your life, rejoice that your goal is secure in Him.

SUMMARY

- Servant leaders accept every experience in their lives as raw material God can use to accomplish His bigger plan.
- God guided Esther's life to preserve Israel while in exile.
- You have a life map that shows how God is at work in your life.
- Though you may feel that you're the unluckiest person in the world, God is at work to move you to your eternal inheritance in Christ Jesus.

1. C. S. Lewis, *The Chronicles of Narnia,* book 5, *The Horse and His Boy* (New York: Collier Books, 1970), 137.

Week 3
LEADERS WHO SERVE, PART 2

This Week's Memory Verse

He said to me, "My grace is sufficient for you, for power is perfected in weakness." Therefore, I will most gladly boast all the more about my weaknesses, so that Christ's power may reside in me.

2 CORINTHIANS 12:9

Tom worked more than 25 years for Big Blue. He saw technology change from punch cards and room-sized computers to CD-ROMs and laptops. IBM trained him in technology and management, project planning and administration. In the early 1990s Tom was part of IBM's paradigm shift toward a consumer-driven company. They trained him to manage change and seek new ways to serve his customers. Tom's vocational skills included managing people, projects, and PCs.

Tom also happened to be the chairman of deacons when I came as the interim pastor of our church in 1986. Tom and his wife loved our church and supported it in many ways. They served in several major ministries through our years together. Tom has a passion for the Lord and His church. Tom is a servant leader.

Tom has a temperament that values high standards. His natural behavioral style is task-oriented, and he seeks to maintain his environment. When he has set a procedure, don't try to change it right away! His commitment to quality and his certainty that quality things will consistently work the same way cause him to question change. When people take time to know Tom and understand the way he relates to others, they see a heart that desires to serve God in the best way possible. Tom sees the world differently than I do. He relates to people differently than I do. We could either be great teammates who complement each other's style or worst enemies who fight to persuade the other to see things our own way. We chose to be teammates.

Several years ago while we were attending a conference together, I asked Tom if he'd ever considered serving God on a local-church staff. He smiled and told me that he'd prayed about that very thing that same morning. He told me about his passion to take his training from business and help a church carry out its ministries more effectively. Later that year Tom left IBM and came to serve our church as the director of planning and administration. After years of service in the local church, he moved to serve in the project-management office in a global evangelistic and missions organization.

Tom offered his temperament, vocational skills, and passion to God for Kingdom service. His life is an example of how God can take someone's relational style with others, skills gained from the marketplace or hobbies, and enthusiasm for ministry and use them to bring honor to Himself.

This Week You Will

- Discover how you relate to others, overview four relational styles, and identify your personal style of relating to others (day 1)
- Compare the relational styles of biblical characters (day 2).
- Take account of the way God uses your vocational skills to accomplish His mission in the world (day 3).
- Inventory the vocational skills that relate to your calling (day 4).
- Understand how God fills you with enthusiasm for ministry (day 5).
- Complete your SERVE profile for the next group session.

God Prepares Servant Leaders to **SERVE**

SPIRITUAL GIFTS

EXPERIENCES

RELATIONAL STYLE

VOCATIONAL SKILLS

ENTHUSIASM

Day 1
RELATING TO OTHERS, PART 1

Leaders have a unique style of leadership, which corresponds
to their temperament and affects how they influence followers.[1]
AUBREY MALPHURS

Today You Will
- Consider relational styles and complete a relational survey.
- Learn how your relational style affects the way you lead.
- Overview four primary relational styles.
- Begin to understand how God has empowered you to overcome conflict
  through an understanding of the relational styles of others.

God Prepares Servant Leaders to SERVE

SPIRITUAL GIFTS

EXPERIENCES

☛ RELATIONAL STYLE

VOCATIONAL SKILLS

ENTHUSIASM

How Does Tom Relate?

I told you about Tom in the introduction to this week's study. Return to
his story and read the way I described his relational style. Record a key
phrase that describes his style.

List the strengths and the weaknesses of Tom's style.

Strengths of Tom's Style   Weaknesses of Tom's Style

Tom's strengths could include a commitment to high standards, loyalty, and the mainte-nance of a steady environment. His weaknesses may include perceived inflexibility and being overly opinionated.

Every person has a natural style for relating to others. Each style has strengths and weaknesses. God can use any relational style that's submitted to His will and His purposes.

The way you relate to others is basic to the way you serve as a leader. To know your relational style is to know the way God has molded you to serve people through your relationships with them. Servant leaders know how they naturally relate to others and how others relate to them.

Because leadership involves influencing others for the common good, knowing how God has molded your temperament is key to knowing your leadership style. Knowing the styles of others also allows you to meet their relational needs. Moreover, understanding the relational needs of others helps you communicate with and lead them more effec-tively. This knowledge will aid you as you equip others (week 4) and team with them in ministry (week 5).

Two words of caution:

1. Your natural relational style isn't an excuse for sinful behavior. It isn't biblical to say, "I'm a dominant person. I tend to run over people. Excuse me if I hurt you." God's Spirit is the balance to your natural style. This week's memory verse, 2 Corinthians 12:9, describes the way God balanced Paul's self-sufficient temperament:

> He said to me, "My grace is sufficient for you, for power is perfected
> in weakness." Therefore, I will most gladly boast all the more about
> my weaknesses, so that Christ's power may reside in me.
> **2 CORINTHIANS 12:9**

God allowed "a thorn in the flesh" (v. 7) to teach Paul that he wasn't as strong as he thought he was. In his weakness Paul discovered the power of God. He learned to boast in his weakness rather than in his accomplishments.

2. To discover your natural relational style doesn't automatically determine how you'll relate in every relationship and situation. God created you a living being, not a machine. You make choices, and your natural style doesn't always predetermine those choices.

God will help you understand your role as a servant leader as you assess the strengths and weaknesses of your relational style. The learning activity that follows is designed to help you do this. It involves the completion of a relational survey that will prove to be a revealing, thought-provoking experience.

The following activity is based on a behavioral theory used often by other Christian writers. This four-category model has been proved over time and has strong scientific support. My primary source for understanding this behavioral theory is the guidance and teaching of my friend Ken Voges, who wrote a book titled *Understanding How Others Misunderstand You.*[2] He created the relational survey included here.

Voges uses the letters DISC to represent four primary relational styles.

Dominance
Influencing
Steadiness
Conscientious

Here's the way these letters compare to another model based on similar theories.

DISC	Smalley/Trent[3]
Dominance	Lion
Influencing	Otter
Steadiness	Golden retriever
Conscientious	Beaver

Plan to spend extra time with this survey. Also plan to spend time today (or later on in the week, if necessary) thinking about what you've discovered and in what ways the survey reflects your own style of servant leadership. Ask yourself, *How does this understanding of myself help me in my role as a servant leader?* You'll have an opportunity to talk about your relational style in your next group session.

Complete the survey as accurately as possible. Some of the choices may be difficult, but do your best to rank each set of terms as they honestly reflect your distinctive, God-given personality. During the group session you won't be asked to share any specific information you wouldn't want to share. Your ranking of each set doesn't reflect a right or wrong choice, nor does it assume that any particular personality style is preferable to another. Your results will give you a picture of strengths you possess that you may never have seen before, and they will help you consider how these strengths can be used in servant leadership.

RELATIONAL SURVEY[4]

Your focus in taking this survey is to select your instinctive behavior and not what you perceive is the best response. There are no right or wrong answers.

Rank each horizontal row of words as either 4, 3, 2, or 1, assigning 4 to the word that *best* describes you and assigning 1 to the word that *least* describes you. Use all rankings in each line only once. Below is an example:

[2] Dominant	[1] Influencing	[4] Steadiness	[3] Conscientious
[ ]	[ ]	[ ]	[ ]
[ ] Forceful	[ ] Lively	[ ] Modest	[ ] Tactful
[ ] Aggressive	[ ] Emotional	[ ] Accommodating	[ ] Consistent
[ ] Direct	[ ] Animated	[ ] Agreeable	[ ] Accurate
[ ] Tough	[ ] People-oriented	[ ] Gentle	[ ] Perfectionist
[ ] Daring	[ ] Impulsive	[ ] Kind	[ ] Cautious
[ ] Competitive	[ ] Expressive	[ ] Supportive	[ ] Precise
[ ] Risk taker	[ ] Talkative	[ ] Relaxed	[ ] Factual
[ ] Argumentative	[ ] Fun-loving	[ ] Patient	[ ] Logical
[ ] Bold	[ ] Spontaneous	[ ] Stable	[ ] Organized
[ ] Take charge	[ ] Optimistic	[ ] Peaceful	[ ] Conscientious
[ ] Candid	[ ] Cheerful	[ ] Loyal	[ ] Serious
[ ] Independent	[ ] Enthusiastic	[ ] Good listener	[ ] High standards
____ TOTAL	____ TOTAL	____ TOTAL	____ TOTAL

If your four totals don't add up to 120, you didn't complete the survey correctly, or you made a mistake in adding up the totals. Recheck your work.

1. Republished under license from In His Grace Inc. Reproduction in any form is prohibited.

TALLYING YOUR SCORE

1. If you haven't added your scores for each of the vertical columns, please do so now. Then, in the large square above the first column, write the letter *D*. Above the second column write *I*, above the third column write *S*, and above the fourth column write *C*. Transfer each of the DISC totals from the bottom of the survey to the boxes below.

D	I	S	C

2. Using these totals, plot your DISC dimensions on the graph shown here; then connect the four points. (See the sample graphs.) This graph will become your personal DISC profile.

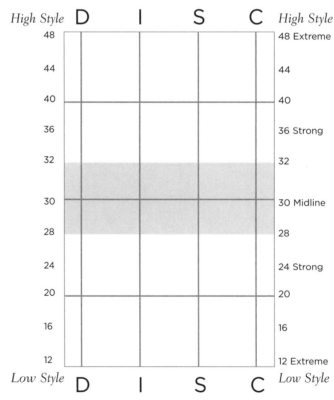

DISC PROFILE

3. After completing the graph, circle all the points above the midline (30). My high style(s) are:

4. On the next page you'll find brief definitions of the four DISC personality styles. Circle the style that you perceive best describes your personality. You probably have characteristics of each of the four styles, but ask yourself, *Which style is most like me?* Circle that style.

SAMPLES

High Dominant   *High Influencing*   *High Steadiness*   *High Conscientious*

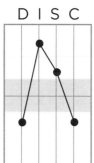 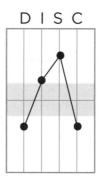 

DEFINITIONS OF DISC STYLES[5]

DOMINANT STYLE. Works toward achieving goals and results; functions best in active, challenging environments

INFLUENCING STYLE. Works toward relating to people through verbal persuasion; functions best in friendly, favorable environments

STEADINESS STYLE. Works toward supporting and cooperating with others; functions best in supportive, harmonious environments

CONSCIENTIOUS STYLE. Works toward doing things right and focuses on details; functions best in structured, orderly environments

How do these descriptions match what was revealed in your DISC profile chart? Consider how your survey results are plotted on the graph. Note not only what's high but also what's low. Ask yourself, *Does this information accurately reflect my personality and the way I see myself relating to others?*

Now personalize your DISC style by completing the following statements.

Because of my style of relating to others, I tend to work toward …

I function best in …

But I also see these additional qualities of my God-given personality:

The most important part of this survey is to reflect on this question: How does my relationship style relate to servant leadership? How can God use the temperament He gave me to make a difference in my church and community?

As you think about these questions, examine the following chart, which summarizes possible strengths and weaknesses of each leadership style.[6]

DOMINANT

Strengths	*Weaknesses*
Direct	Too controlling
Active	Hates routine
Decisive	Hates details

INFLUENCING

Strengths	*Weaknesses*
Gregarious	Not remembering the goal
Enthusiastic	Poor follow-through
Extremely flexible	Overlooks details

STEADINESS

Strengths	*Weaknesses*
Cooperative	Fails to confront
Deliberate	Dislikes change
Supportive	Too compromising

CONSCIENTIOUS

Strengths	*Weaknesses*
Detailed	Inflexible
Conscientious	Rigid
Cautious	Indecisive

Note that each style has both strengths and weaknesses. No single style can meet every need. God intentionally created a variety of styles, none being more important or more needed than another. All gifts and strengths are important to the overall servant ministry of your church. At the same time, each strength, when out of control, can become a weakness. And weaknesses shouldn't become excuses for failure. A person and a church must constantly strive to accomplish without excuse the ministries assigned by God.

This diversity of styles in a church may at times produce conflict, but it provides the important balance needed to accomplish what God gives the church to do. It reminds us of the important lesson that God needs each one of us and that we need one another.

Circle the words or phrases in the previous chart that best describe you. This is an opportunity to remind yourself of who you are in Christ and to think about ways He can use you in servant ministry. Honestly be grateful for your strengths and objectively consider the weaknesses you need to overcome.

As you consider the strengths and weaknesses listed on this chart, it may be interesting to think about your spouse or a close friend you work with. How does God use your different styles to complement each other?

A Story of Change

A church member sat across from me in my office. He had called earlier that afternoon and said he needed to talk. I knew some of the changes we'd made in our worship services and church organization had been a concern for him. We'd made major changes to our worship style in the past months. We'd also changed our church organization to make decisions more quickly and effectively.

Change comes easily for me. I see it as part of life. You know the old saying "The only thing that doesn't change is change." Growing things change. Change is a sign of health and life. Churches that change, I reason, are healthy. Churches that won't change, I feel, are dead. If we aren't growing, we're dying. I soon discovered that not everyone agrees with me.

As my friend sat down, he said he wanted to share his heart with me. I listened as he told me that the changes in recent months were too much for him. Change had happened too quickly. People were upset and confused, he felt. (I also knew in his company had gone through a major reorganization and his children were preparing to leave home. Change had become the only constant in his life.) He told me his family felt they needed to start looking for another church. He said, "Gene, everything in my life is changing. I don't want my church to change too." I shared again why I thought the changes were needed. I shared that I believed God was reviving His church to reach the next generation and that these changes were part of that revival. He told me of his desire for predictability in the services and some sense of tradition. I stressed the need for variety and new traditions.

We talked for a long time. We prayed and hugged, and he left. I stood alone in my office wondering where I'd gone wrong.

As I look back on that conversation, I realized my friend taught me that people respond to change based on their temperament as much as on their theology. He wanted a predictable, steady church experience. I accepted variety and change. Neither one of us was wrong. We simply desired different things based on the way God had wired us. I've found that many conflicts result more from the way we naturally relate to others—which affects the way we see the world—than from wrong theology. Conflict most often occurs when we push our natural tendencies to extremes. When this happens, strengths become weaknesses.

You may have had a similar experience with a friend or a church member. You simply see things differently than the other person. You remain friends because you love the person more than you disagree with his or her preferences. Churches function best when members accept the relational styles of others and seek to meet the needs of those people, while never compromising the message of Christ. Relationships remain strong when church members follow God's pattern for living together as His body with all its diversity (see 1 Cor. 12:14-26).

God's Word offers clear teaching on serving one another in love:

> God's chosen ones, holy and loved, put on heartfelt compassion, kindness, humility, gentleness, and patience, accepting one another and forgiving one another if anyone has a complaint against another. Just as the Lord has forgiven you, so you must also forgive. Above all, put on love—the perfect bond of unity.
> **COLOSSIANS 3:12-14**

Circle the "clothing" you're to wear as a chosen child of God.

What should be your standard for forgiveness?

What's the virtue that creates "the perfect bond of unity" (v. 14)?

As a servant leader, you should be sensitive to others' relational needs and serve them by loving and forgiving as Christ loved and forgave you.

Take a moment and ask God to give you the name of someone with whom you currently have conflict. Seek to understand the differences in relational styles that may have contributed to the conflict. Ask God to clothe you in His love and give you the grace to forgive this person with the forgiveness with which He has forgiven you. Resolve to go to that person this week and seek forgiveness, keeping in mind Paul's admonition:

Decide never to put a stumbling block or pitfall in your brother's way.
ROMANS 14:13

Remember that your natural relational style isn't an excuse to sin. God's indwelling Spirit balances your natural tendencies with God's temperament. Regardless of your style, the fruit of the Spirit is always a vital part of a servant leader's relationships:

The fruit of the Spirit is love, joy, peace, patience, kindness, goodness, faith, gentleness, self-control. Against such things there is no law.
GALATIANS 5:22-23

God's Spirit molds your temperament for His glory.

SUMMARY

- You have a natural style for relating to others.
- There are four primary relational styles. Each style has both strengths and weaknesses.
- Conflict happens when people's natural styles cause differences of opinion and/or are pushed to an extreme.
- God's Word teaches that you're to be compassionate and forgiving to those with whom you may have conflict.
- God's Holy Spirit is the balance to your natural style.

---

1. Aubrey Malphurs, *Being Leaders: The Nature of Authentic Christian Leadership,* Kindle edition (Ada, MI: Baker Publishing Group, 2003), 79.
2. Ken Voges and Ron Braund, *Understanding How Others Misunderstand You* (Chicago: Moody Press, 1990). A workbook by the same title contains two personality assessment tests and studies ideal for retreats and small groups. Ken is responsible for the biblical content in Performax Biblical Personal Profile, available from Carlson Learning Company. I am indebted to Ken for his insights into the biblical characters portrayed in this week's study. Copies of *Understanding How Others Misunderstand You* book and workbook can be obtained through In His Grace Inc.; 3006 Quincannon; Houston, TX 77043; phone 713.934.8810; fax 713.462.2208; visit *http://inhisgraceinc.com*.
3. Gary Smalley and John Trent, *The Two Sides of Love* (Pomona, CA: Focus on the Family Publishing, 1990), 34–36.
4. The relational survey included in today's study is adapted from DISC Relationship Survey and Team Building Survey, published by In His Grace Inc., Houston, TX, copyright 1995. Used by permission. This assessment survey is designed to determine your general DISC styles. For a more complete analysis refer to *Understanding How Others Misunderstand You Workbook*. Information on training seminars, technical support, and stand-alone DISC surveys on relationships, team building, parenting, and conflict resolution can be obtained through In His Grace Inc.; 3006 Quincannon; Houston, TX 77043; phone 713.934.8810; fax 713.462.2208.
5. Ibid.
6. Ibid.

Day 2
RELATING TO OTHERS, PART 2

Today You Will
- Examine examples of each of the four relational styles.
- Observe the way Jesus showed the strengths of each relational style.
- Compare relational styles.

Yesterday you learned about the four primary relational styles. You discovered the strengths and weaknesses of each style and how those strengths and weaknesses influence leadership. You completed a relational survey to discover your primary relational style. Today you'll compare your relational style with that of a well-known Bible character. You'll observe ways God used this person's personality, and you'll consider ways He can also use your style to make a difference in the world.

Let's look now at the lives of biblical leaders to discover ways God has used individuals like you to accomplish His purposes.

Paul: A Dominant Leader

Paul was a servant leader whom God chose to serve the mission of God in a special way. Let's observe Paul's relational style and discover ways God used and molded it for His service. Search the following passages to learn how Paul related to others.

In Galatians 2:11-19a Paul was writing to the churches in Galatia to address a heresy challenging salvation through faith alone.

Read Galatians 2:11-19a. Whom did Paul address in this passage (see v. 11)?

What was the tone of his message (see vv. 11,14)?

Do you think there was any room for compromise in his comments (see vv. 15-16)?   Yes   No

In Acts 15:36-41 Paul wanted to go back to the churches that were established on his first missionary journey. He invited Barnabas to go with him, and Barnabas wanted to include John Mark on the journey.

> **Read Acts 15:36-41. Why didn't Paul want to take John Mark (see v. 38)?**
>
> **How does the Bible describe their disagreement (see v. 39)?**
>
> **What did Paul decide to do (see v. 40)?**
>
> **Describe your perception of Paul's relational style as he related to others.**
>
> **List the strengths and weaknesses of Paul's style.**
>
> **Strengths of Paul's Style   Weaknesses of Paul's Style**

Paul's strengths included his commitment to the task God assigned to him, his determination in tough situations, and his decisiveness. His weaknesses included a controlling spirit and a tendency to ignore people's feelings. God used Paul's dominant style to lead the new mission to carry the gospel around the world to all people.

Sarah, Abraham's wife, is a feminine example of the dominant relational style. She suggested that Abraham take her handmaid in order to gain the inheritance of God's promise (see Gen. 16:1-2). Later she insisted that Abraham remove Hagar and her son from the camp (see 21:10).

Jesus: A Dominant Leader

Jesus was the perfect human. In His life on earth He displayed the positive strengths of each behavioral style, and He never violated God's law as He modeled these relational styles. In John 8:12-59 Jesus displayed a dominant leadership style as He confronted the religious leaders of His day,[1] who challenged Jesus' witness about Himself. Jesus confronted their thinking by teaching that they judged by human standards and knew nothing of Him:

"Even if I testify about Myself," Jesus replied, "My testimony
is valid, because I know where I came from and where I'm
going. But you don't know where I come from or where
I'm going. You judge by human standards. I judge no one.
JOHN 8:14-15

Jesus declared that His testimony was true because He and His Father were one, and Their
witness was valid:

If I do judge, My judgment is true, because I am not alone, but I and
the Father who sent Me judge together. Even in your law it is written
that the witness of two men is valid. I am the One who testifies about
Myself, and the Father who sent Me testifies about Me." Then they asked
Him, "Where is Your Father?" "You know neither Me nor My Father,"
Jesus answered. "If you knew Me, you would also know My Father.
JOHN 8:16-19

Jesus refused to back down as the religious leaders challenged Him.

Barnabas: An Influencing Leader

We meet Barnabas early in the Book of Acts. He was a Levite from the island of Cyprus.
His name was Joseph, but the apostles called him Barnabas, which means "Son of
Encouragement" (Acts 4:36). We learn that he had a generous heart and shared his pos-
sessions with the church (see v. 37).

In Acts 9:23-28 Jesus had just called Saul of Tarsus to a ministry to the Gentiles.
Paul began to preach in Damascus, but he fled to Jerusalem when some religious leaders
planned to kill him.

**Read Acts 9:23-28. What did the believers in Jerusalem think of Saul
(see v. 26)?**

Who encouraged the disciples to trust Saul (see v. 27)?

What was the result of Barnabas's intervention (see v. 28)?

Return to Acts 15:36-41. Read the passage from Barnabas's point of view.

Why do you think Barnabas wanted to take John Mark with him?

Why do you think Paul and Barnabas made such a good team?

Why do you think they broke up their ministry team?

Describe the relational style of Barnabas.

List the strengths and weaknesses of Barnabas's relational style.

Strengths of Barnabas's Style	Weaknesses of Barnabas's Style

The strengths of Barnabas's personality included his outgoing nature, enthusiasm, and flexibility. His weaknesses included poor follow-through and a strong need to please others.

Abigail is a female example of the influencing relational style. Abigail, the wife of Nabal (see 1 Sam. 25), used her natural skills of influencing and gift giving to soothe David's anger and thus prevented David and his men from killing Nabal. After Nabal's death Abigail became David's wife.

Jesus: An Influencing Leader

Jesus also modeled the positive characteristics of an influencing style. When He came to the well in Samaria, He persuasively and sensitively approached the woman there (see John 4:1-42).[2] As she asked about water and where people should worship, Jesus gently guided her to Himself, the Living Water. Jesus influenced her to trust in Him. He confronted her sin without damaging her already-hurting heart.

Abraham: A Steady Leader

God chose Abraham to be the father of His chosen people (see Gen. 12:1-3). God called Abraham from his homeland and sent him into the promised land of Canaan. As we see Abraham follow God's leadership, several events along the way reveal Abraham's relational style. The first is seen when he went to Egypt because of a famine in the land.

Read Genesis 12:10-20. What did Abraham suggest that Sarah do to avoid conflict with the Egyptians (see vv. 11-13)?

What does this incident say about Abraham's relational style?

God made a covenant with Abraham that He would make his descendants outnumber the stars in the sky (see 15:1-6). The only problem was that Abraham had no descendants, and he and Sarah were very old.

Read Genesis 16:1-6. This passage describes Abraham's relational style with his wife, Sarah. Who made the suggestion to have a child by Hagar, the Egyptian maidservant (see vv. 1-2)?

What was Abraham's response to this suggestion (see vv. 3-4)?

What do these verses say about Abraham's relational style with his wife?

Abraham clearly didn't like conflict. He preferred harmony, the status quo, and security in relationships. He didn't like pain, change, and insecurity, but his trust in God allowed him to overcome these natural tendencies to avoid uncertainty. His willingness to sacrifice Isaac, his only physical hope of God's covenant, proved this fact (see 22:1-19).

Abraham's faith is the reason he was honored in Scripture. The writer of Hebrews described this man of faith this way:

By faith Abraham, when he was called, obeyed and went
out to a place he was going to receive as an inheritance.
He went out, not knowing where he was going.
HEBREWS 11:8

Although Abraham's tendency was for steadiness in life and in relationships, God used him to father the nation of Israel and to settle the promised land.

Describe Abraham's relational style.

List the strengths and weaknesses of Abraham's style.

Strengths of Abraham's Style	Weaknesses of Abraham's Style

Abraham's strengths included a cooperative spirit, deliberate actions, and a supportive attitude. He may be perceived to be weak because he failed to confront others, disliked change, and was often overly compromising.

Hannah, the mother of Samuel, is a female example of the steadiness relational style. Hannah was unable to bear children. Even under harassment from a rival wife who bore children, Hannah didn't retaliate but faithfully prayed to God (see 1 Sam. 1:10-11). When God answered her prayer, she followed through with her promise and dedicated her son to the work of God (see vv. 24-28).

Jesus: A Steady Leader

Jesus also showed the strengths of a steadiness style in His relationships with others. When the religious leaders brought to Him the woman caught in adultery, He defused the situation by drawing attention away from her and to Himself (see John 8:1-9). He removed the tension before He taught a lesson. This incident showed Jesus' ability to relate steadily to those who confronted Him without resorting to lying like Abraham.[3]

Moses: A Conscientious Leader

God chose Moses to lead His covenant people out of bondage. God also called him to record the Ten Commandments. God's choice required a special kind of person. Let's look at some events in Moses' life that reveal his natural relational style and ways God used him for His purposes.

> **Read Exodus 2:11-20. What did Moses do when he saw an Egyptian beating a fellow countryman (see v. 12)?**
>
> **When Moses fled to Midian, what did he do when the shepherds chased off the priest's daughters (see v. 17)?**
>
> **What do these two incidents tell you about Moses' natural relational style?**

In Exodus 32 God had led Israel out of Egypt. The people were camped at the foot of Mount Sinai, and Moses was on the mountain talking with God. The people became restless and had Aaron create a golden calf (see vv. 1-6). They began to worship it.

> **Read Exodus 32:19-29. What did Moses do when he came off the mountain and saw what the people were doing?**
>
> **What does this incident say about Moses' commitment to God's laws?**

> **Read Exodus 34:4-9. God had told Moses He would reveal Himself to him. What did God say about Himself when He passed in front of Moses on the mountain (see vv. 6-7)?**

God revealed these attributes to Moses to balance his own high standards of holiness. Moses needed to know the compassion of God while maintaining the holiness of God. Moses responded in worship (see vv. 8-9).

Describe Moses' relational style.

List the strengths and weaknesses of Moses' style.

Strengths of Moses' Style	Weaknesses of Moses' Style

Moses' strengths included his concern for justice, his attention to detail, and his high moral standards. Weaknesses of his relational style included inflexibility, rigidity, and indecisiveness.

Esther is a feminine example of the conscientious relational style. Esther became the queen after being chosen from among the women of Persia. When Mordecai, her cousin, told her about a plot to kill the Jews, her first response was to state the rules for approaching the king (see Esth. 4:11). Yet when she understood the opportunity God had given her to save His people, she boldly entered the king's presence. God used this woman to preserve the people of Israel.

Jesus: A Conscientious Leader

Jesus modeled the strengths of this relational style as well. When asked about Scripture, He defended the authority of God's Word. In a debate with the religious leaders of His day, He clearly stated God's intention in Scripture (see Matt. 22:23-46). Jesus conscientiously conformed to God's standards of holiness as He taught those who questioned Him.[4]

God Uses People for His Purposes

God used the temperaments of Paul, Barnabas, Abraham, and Moses to accomplish His purposes in the world. God used Paul's dominant style to face conflict and challenges while on mission. God used Barnabas's influencing style to bring Paul into the church and to heal hurt people like John Mark. God used Abraham's steadiness to teach faith. God used Moses' high standards to record His perfect law. God used these servant leaders' natural relational styles to carry out His plan in the world. God also empowered them with His power, His presence, and His Word to do more than their natural capabilities would allow.

God provides people with a variety of relational styles to balance the church's ministry teams. We need one another. God used the domineering Paul and the influencing Barnabas to do His will in carrying the gospel of Jesus around the world. Their strengths complemented each other, and those same strengths, pushed to an extreme, caused a broken relationship. The same results can occur in today's churches and ministries.

A Comparison of Relational Styles

Now that you've observed the relational styles of Paul and Sarah, Barnabas and Abigail, Abraham and Hannah, and Moses and Esther, ask yourself, *Which person's style is most similar to my own?*

Look back at the strengths and weaknesses you listed for each biblical character, as well as the DISC profiles here, which show possible profiles of these four distinct personalities.[5] Review your own profile, which you completed yesterday, to determine whether it matches the possible profile of Paul, Barnabas, Abraham, or Moses.

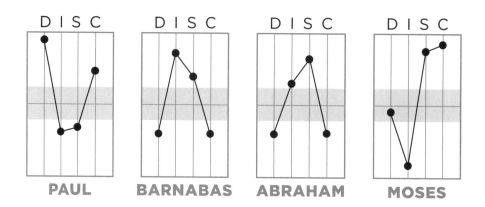

Choose the style that's most like you.

____ Paul and Sarah   ____ Barnabas and Abigail

____ Abraham and Hannah   ____ Moses and Esther

As you reflect on your activities in this workbook this week, keep in mind that these patterns and interpretations are based on a behavioral profile only—without information about intelligence, personal values, versatility, and other factors that could affect your behavior. Again, no particular pattern is good, bad, or better than another. Knowing your typical pattern should provide you with insights that will enable you to understand yourself and others in a way that maximizes your potential and your abilities as an effective servant leader of Christ.[6]

SUMMARY

- God used Paul's dominant style to spread the gospel around the world.
- God used Barnabas's influencing style to build the first missionary team and to restore John Mark to the church's mission.
- God used Abraham to teach biblical faith.
- God used Moses to present His laws to His people.
- God can empower and provide others in the church to balance your natural style for His purposes.

1. Ken Voges and Ron Braund, *Understanding How Others Misunderstand You* (Chicago: Moody Press. 1990), 271.
2. Ken Voges and Mike Kempainen, *Understanding Jesus* (Chicago: Moody Press, 1992), 24.
3. Voges and Braund, *Understanding How Others Misunderstand You Workbook,* 110.
4. Ibid.
5. Graphs taken from *Understanding How Others Misunderstand You* by Ken Voges and Ron Braund. Copyright © 1990, 1995, Moody Bible Institute of Chicago. Moody Press. Used by permission.
6. Ibid., 132.

Day 3
VOCATIONAL SKILLS, PART 1

A career is something I choose for myself; a calling is
something I receive. A career is something I do for myself;
a calling is something I do for God. ... A career is about upward
mobility; a calling generally leads to downward mobility.[1]
JOHN ORTBERG

Today You Will
- Consider the meaning of vocation as it relates to your SERVE profile.
- Observe how God used the vocations of those He called to support their calling.
- Assess your vocational skills as they relate to your role as a servant leader.

God Prepares Servant Leaders to SERVE

SPIRITUAL GIFTS

EXPERIENCES

RELATIONAL STYLE

☛ VOCATIONAL SKILLS

ENTHUSIASM

What Is a Vocational Skill?

When you think of vocation, what comes to your mind?

Our English word *vocation* comes from the Latin *vocare,* which means *to call.* A vocation is what someone feels called to do with his or her life. In previous generations a sense of divine calling was part of a person's place in the world. A vocation was part of God's plan for a person's life. God called, and a person responded by gaining the skills necessary to live out that calling. Today vocation has come to mean any profession or occupation. A vocational skill is any ability you've learned that enhances your calling in life.

In today's secular world people often prefer to use the word *career* for their vocation. A career is your choice. Instead of looking for God's plan, the world teaches you to choose what you want to do and then to plot a course of training to accomplish your career choice. A career, then, is what you choose for yourself. A calling, according to Scripture, is God's invitation to join Him in His mission of reconciling people to Himself and to give your whole being to that calling.

In the New Testament Paul encouraged the Christians in Ephesus "to walk worthy of the calling you have received" (Eph. 4:1). He wasn't talking about their jobs. He encouraged them to adopt a lifestyle consistent with who they were in Christ. Calling in the Bible is a person's position in Christ, not a person's position in the world.

Whatever your vocation, your calling is to live worthy of the salvation God gives you in Christ Jesus. In his letter to the Colossians, Paul wrote:

> Whatever you do, do it enthusiastically, as something done
> for the Lord and not for men. ... You serve the Lord Christ.
> **COLOSSIANS 3:23-24**

Whatever you do, God calls you to live like a child of God and to bring honor to God through your actions. It matters less what you do in life than what you do with your life.

For the sake of our study, let's define *vocation* as what you do to provide for your needs in society, recognizing God's work in your life to lead you to that choice. *Calling* is God's call to salvation in Christ Jesus and to a special mission in your life for His purposes.

Read the passages and record the biblical characters' vocation (what they did for a living) and calling (what God asked them to do).

	Vocation	God's Calling
Moses (see Ex. 3:1-10)		
Simon Peter (see Mark 1:16-18)		
Paul (see Acts 9:1-16; 18:1-3)		
Lydia (see Acts 16:14-15,40)		

Moses was a shepherd who led his sheep to food and water and provided them protection; God called him to lead His people out of bondage. Peter was a fisherman; God called him to follow Jesus and become a fisher of men. Paul made tents; God called him to use that vocation to support himself as he carried the good news to the world. Lydia sold fabric; God called her to use her resources to support the mission to the Gentiles.

God called people to join Him in reconciling the world to Himself through His Son, Jesus. God used their vocations to fulfill that calling.

Jesus Was a Carpenter

We don't always consider Jesus as a person with a career. However, until He stepped into the public eye at age 30, He had a vocation as a carpenter (see Mark 6:3), following in the footsteps of His earthly father, Joseph. We can only speculate what Jesus did as a carpenter. Perhaps God used times when Jesus created needed tools and furniture from unhewn trees to remind Jesus of His power and joy in the act of creation. Mending broken items that were brought to Him reflected Jesus' desire to mend the broken hearts of people. Jesus was well known in His hometown (see 6:1-6), perhaps because Jesus went about kindly helping others through His vocation of carpentry. God placed Jesus in the home of a carpenter to teach Him a trade and to mold His heart for servant ministry.

A Personal Story

A pivotal moment in my life came when I realized I could have any job and still live out God's calling in my life. In week 2 I shared with you God's call in my life to pursue a full-time Christian vocation. I was convinced that God wanted me to be a pastor. My temperament and models for ministry guided me to be the guy up front. After I graduated from college and got married, I joined the staff of a suburban church as a pastoral intern. This role was ideal as I began seminary. I soon found myself spending most of my time with youth. My wife was a middle-school and high-school teacher, so the fit was perfect. In 1979, the year I began my PhD studies, this church of three thousand members asked me to be its youth minister. My wife and church family sensed this was what God wanted us to do, so we jumped in with both feet.

After three years of full-time ministry and as I finished my doctoral work, a college friend called and asked me to consider heading up a private foundation that ministered through camps and conference centers. We'd dreamed together about a camping ministry that could help youth in need, and youth summer camp was always the high point of my year. I sensed God wanted me to do youth ministry full-time. Again, my wife and church family sensed this was what God wanted me to do. It was a hard decision. How could I be a pastor, as God had called me to be, and the executive director of an unknown, private foundation? I felt I was leaving God's call.

After I finished my doctoral degree, I soon found myself frustrated as I taught a Sunday School class with a degree in New Testament studies and hung out with students on ropes courses at our camps. How could I be doing what God had called me to do? This didn't make sense.

One day as I sat quietly on the side of a mountain outside a Colorado camp, I opened my heart to God. I prayed, "Why haven't You made me a pastor? I have my degrees and experience. I know I can do the job. Why haven't You let me do what I thought You called me to do 16 years ago?" I was really upset.

Then the still, small voice of the Spirit said, "Gene, you can be a mail carrier and do what I called you to do." I listened longer. God's Spirit pointed out that the position I held had little to do with His hold on my life. The Spirit continued, "Be faithful to the task at hand." Romans 8:28 came to mind, and I sensed God knew how all this was working together for His good. That day I separated God's calling from my career. I didn't have to be in my chosen position to be part of God's calling for my life. I realized God can use anybody in any job to do His will. I breathed a sigh of relief and gladly went down the hill to lead a Bible study for a group of high-school students.

I've eventually seen my calling and career merge. God, not I, decided when and how they would come together. God taught me that whether you're a mail carrier or a preacher, He calls you to follow Him. God's call to follow Him has priority over your choice of careers. But whatever your career, God can use you to complete His plan for your life.

What's Your Story?

What God calls you to do is made clear throughout the Bible. Many people have stressed the Great Commandment (Mark 12:29-31) and the Great Commission (Matt. 28:19-20) as starting points for discerning God's call on your life as a follower of Jesus:

> "This is the most important," Jesus answered: " 'Listen, Israel!
> The Lord our God, the Lord is One. Love the Lord your God
> with all your heart, with all your soul, with all your mind, and
> with all your strength.' The second is: 'Love your neighbor as
> yourself.' There is no other command greater than these."
> **MARK 12:29-31**

Go, therefore, and make disciples of all nations, baptizing them
in the name of the Father and of the Son and of the Holy Spirit,
teaching them to observe everything I have commanded you.
And remember, I am with you always, to the end of the age.
MATTHEW 28:19-20

In Christ God calls you to live for Him in every area of your life. God may use your vocation to enhance His call in your life. When you take this higher view of your life in Christ Jesus, God's calling takes precedence over any choice of jobs.

Record what you believe God has called you to do with your life.

You also may have chosen a career. Describe your career choice and why you made it.

Now reflect on God's calling and your career choices. List ways your calling and career can complement and serve each other.

Tomorrow we'll look at specific vocational skills you have that God can use to enhance His calling in your life.

SUMMARY

- A vocation is what you do to provide for your needs in society.
- A vocational skill is any ability you've learned to enhance your career in life.
- Calling in the Bible is a person's position in Christ, not a person's position in the world.
- Calling is God's call to salvation in Christ Jesus and to a special mission for His purposes.
- God can use the skills you've acquired as part of your career to complete His calling in your life.

1. John Ortberg, *If You Want to Walk on Water, You've Got to Get Our of the Boat* (Grand Rapids: Zondervan, 2001), 71.

Day 4
VOCATIONAL SKILLS, PART 2

Today You Will

- Observe how God used two of Paul's vocational skills to further His mission.
- Read the story of one person who uses his skills to do the will of God.
- Inventory skills you can use in service to God.

Paul's Vocational Skills

God prepared Paul with two unique vocational skills while He was still Saul—before He called him to witness to the Gentile world. These skills—interpreting Scripture and tent making—directly related to God's call for Paul to be a messenger of the gospel.

Read Philippians 3:5-6. What was Paul's career before his conversion?

What skills do you think he acquired in this position?

1. INTERPRETING SCRIPTURE. Growing up in a Jewish home, Saul memorized important parts of the Old Testament (see Acts 26:4-6). He went to Jerusalem to train as a Pharisee. There he learned the Old Testament law, its interpretation, and how his sect of Judaism translated Scripture into daily life. He learned the biblical language of Hebrew along with his native dialect of Aramaic. He learned to read the Greek Old Testament (the Septuagint). Saul was trained in debate. He was zealously loyal to the oral traditions taught by his teacher, Gamaliel (see 22:3). Saul's vocational training as a Pharisee prepared him to understand Scripture and to recognize who Jesus was and why He came.

Read Galatians 3:10-14, Paul's argument for justification by faith.
How many Old Testament verses did he use in that passage?

How did knowing the Old Testament law and Jewish methods of interpreting it help Paul explain justification by faith to his readers?

God gave Saul the skills to interpret the Old Testament before He made him Paul, the apostle. In his discussion about justification by faith, he quoted the Old Testament four times in verses 10-13. God used Paul's skills and His Word to explain His plan for salvation to all people.

2. TENT MAKING. God used a second vocational skill that aided Paul in his calling. As part of his religious training, he learned a trade. We don't learn until Paul was on his missionary journeys that his trade was tent making (see Acts 18:2-3). The term referred more generally to someone who worked with leather. In Paul's day teachers and scribes commonly had a trade to support themselves in addition to their study and teaching of the law.

Read 1 Corinthians 9:1-15. What arguments did Paul use to support a teacher's right to receive gifts for his labor?

Why did Paul refused to accept payment for his ministry?

Paul said he had every right to accept money for his teaching. He and his companions refused to exercise those rights "so that we will not hinder the gospel of Christ" (v. 12). In verse 15 he reiterated that he hadn't used any of his rights as a teacher to accept money:

> I have used none of these rights, and I have not written this
> to make it happen that way for me. For it would be better
> for me to die than for anyone to deprive me of my boast!
> **1 CORINTHIANS 9:15**

Read 1 Thessalonians 2:9. Paul defended himself to the Christians in Thessalonica by saying he didn't take material support from them:

> You remember our labor and hardship, brothers.
> Working night and day so that we would not burden
> any of you, we preached God's gospel to you.
> **1 THESSALONIANS 2:9**

What did Paul do to avoid requiring material support?

Paul's vocational skill of tent making provided an income and a platform for his calling to preach the gospel to all people. When he arrived in a city, he rented a booth for his trade and reasoned "in the marketplace every day with those who happened to be there" (Acts 17:17). Paul learned this skill before God called him. Then God used his acquired skill to carry the gospel around the world. If you follow Paul's missionary journeys, you find that his longest stays were in major trading centers. Corinth and Ephesus both provided marketplaces and sufficient populations for him to use his skill to support God's call in his life.

God allowed Paul to learn how to interpret Scripture and make tents. Then God introduced him to His Son, Jesus. After that Paul's vocational skills took a new direction.

A Present-Day Story

Kenny is a Chinese-born Christian and an American citizen who married an American missionary while she served in China. He earned his master's degree in business from a major Chinese University after he'd committed his life to the Lord. As part of his master's work, he had to design a plan for a viable business. In the mid-1990s the ability to speak English and use a computer were rare commodities among the Chinese people where he grew up and lived. His plan was to create a computer and English learning center that would provide training to students and adults. His plan was approved, and Kenny and his wife, June, opened the center. In the summers they invited English-speaking Christians from the United States to teach the English classes. They honored the laws of the land and didn't present the gospel in class, but in conversations before and after classes the teachers bridged the dialogue to religion, atheism, and trust in Jesus.

For more than 10 years this couple, their staff, and invited teachers invested their vocational skills of teaching English as a second language and computer skills as a platform to lead others to trust in Jesus. Some of my favorite memories of church in a country that opposed it was with that couple and the Chinese Christians who came to trust Jesus as their Rescuer and Lord. Kenny and June later came to lead the English language and citizenship programs at the church I pastored, and many more internationals came to trust Jesus through their work.

Your Vocational Skills

Vocational skills are skills you've acquired to carry out your career and/or hobbies.

Make an inventory of your skills.

Name of Skill   **How I Use This Skill in My Vocation**

Your Skills for God's Calling

Now that you've inventoried your major vocational skills, imagine how God can use those skills in His work of spreading the gospel and making disciples. For example, if one of your skills is carpentry, you can use that skill to build shelves in your church's preschool rooms or for a local mission or ministry.

List skills below that you can use in God's mission. Be creative as you consider ways you can use your skills for the glory of God.

Name of Skill   **How God Can Use This Skill in His Mission**

SUMMARY

- God prepared Paul with unique vocational skills before He called him to witness to the Gentile world.
- Paul's vocational training as a Pharisee prepared him to use Scripture to tell who Jesus was and why He came.
- Paul's vocational skill of tent making provided income and a platform for his calling to preach the gospel.
- Like Paul's skills, your vocational skills can be transformed to serve God's Kingdom purposes.

Day 5
ENTHUSIASM

When passion and a clear idea are wed, the passion can more
easily spread. Cascading contagion requires clarity first.[1]
WILL MANCINI

Today You Will
- Define *enthusiasm* and discover how it relates to you as a servant leader.
- Observe the role enthusiasm played in the life of Apollos.
- Identify ways John the Baptist modeled biblical passion as well as the principle
  of servant leadership.
- Complete a SERVE profile.

God Prepares Servant Leaders to SERVE

SPIRITUAL GIFTS

EXPERIENCES

RELATIONAL STYLE

VOCATIONAL SKILLS

☞ ENTHUSIASM

Have you ever met someone who was truly excited about what he or she was doing?
Nothing seemed to get them down. They were eager to do their job, and you could sense
it. *Enthusiasm* means *an intense or eager interest*. You may say, "Sarah is enthusiastic about
her ministry to families. She lights up every time she tells you about it." Enthusiastic
people make service enjoyable.

Make a list of enthusiastic people you know. Then answer the question: What in their behavior signals enthusiasm?

Enthusiastic People I Know   **What They Do**

The word *enthusiasm* comes from a Greek word meaning *in god*. The Greeks believed a god could enter a person and inspire or enthuse him. Our word *enthusiasm* takes on the meaning *God in you*. Although the Greek word for *enthuse* isn't found in the New Testament, the emphasis on God's presence energizing a believer is a recurring theme (see Matt. 28:18-20; John 14:20; 20:21-22; Acts 1:8). The Bible is clear that God's Holy Spirit is the source of passion for God's mission within the believer. Paul declared that "Christ in you" is "the hope of glory" (Col. 1:27). We don't generate hope on our own. God energizes us with His living Holy Spirit. Jesus promised that the Holy Spirit will be our Counselor and "guide [us] into all the truth" (John 16:13) as we follow the Lord. Passion and enthusiasm for ministry come from God.

Scripture tells about people who were enthusiastic about what they did. This isn't a self-generated thrill. As it relates to this study, enthusiasm is a God-given desire to serve Him by meeting the needs of others. Servant leaders have a God-given passion to serve. Today we we'll observe three people who were servant leaders and were enthusiastic about their service to God. We'll also see how they differed in their passion for God's work.

Jesus: An Enthusiastic Leader

Jesus was filled with a confidence and enthusiasm about His ministry. People were drawn to Him because of His passion for life and ministry. Jesus taught with enthusiasm. The Bible states that after the Sermon on the Mount:

> The crowds were astonished at His teaching, because
> He was teaching them like one who had authority.
> **MATTHEW 7:28-29**

We get a glimpse of Jesus' passion for His disciples as He told them:

> Your heart must not be troubled. Believe in God; believe also in Me.
> **JOHN 14:1**

We see Jesus' all-consuming passion to do God's will when He declared:

> I have come down from heaven, not to do My will, but the will of Him who sent Me. This is the will of Him who sent Me: that I should lose none of those He has given Me but should raise them up on the last day.
> **JOHN 6:38-39**

Jesus was filled with passion for His mission, and it showed!

Apollos: A Passionate Teacher

Read Acts 18:24-26. Where was Apollos from?

How does the Bible describe his skills and enthusiasm?

Apollos came from the ancient intellectual center of Alexandria in Egypt. This city was the home of the Greek translation of the Old Testament. Luke tells us that Apollos was "an eloquent man who was powerful in the use of the Scriptures" (v. 24). He'd been taught in the way of the Lord, and he spoke with great fervor. The Bible says he boldly taught about Jesus, but his teaching was incomplete. He knew only the baptism of John, a baptism of repentance.

The phrase that described Apollos's teaching, "fervent in spirit" (v. 25), is a translation of the idiom "to boil in the spirit."[2] Apollos loved to teach about Jesus. He boldly preached about Jesus in Ephesus, where Paul had left Priscilla and Aquila.

By itself, however, Apollos' enthusiasm didn't lend itself to an effective ministry of the gospel. He knew only of the baptism of John. His passion was full, but his facts weren't straight. Proverbs warns:

> Even zeal is not good without knowledge.
> **PROVERBS 19:2**

Enthusiasm alone doesn't make you a servant leader. Luke tells us that Priscilla and Aquila took Apollos into their home and "explained the way of God to him more accurately." (Acts 18:26). What the two more mature Christians did is called mentoring. A Christlike spirit and a deep desire to learn with a servant's heart must accompany passion.

John the Baptist:
A Passionate Servant Leader

Read John 3:22-30. What does verse 23 say about the success of John's ministry?

Some of John's disciples came to him and pointed to the success of another. How did John respond?

How would you characterize John's response?

John first noted that success comes only from God (see v. 27). If people were swarming to Jesus, it was part of God's plan. John also restated the fact that he wasn't the Messiah. He was sent ahead of God's Chosen One to prepare the way of the Lord (see v. 28). Then John drew an analogy from everyday life, pointing out that only the bridegroom gets the bride. The friend who attends the bridegroom is usually the groom's best friend. His joy and job are complete when he leads the bride to the bridegroom (see v. 29). John said his joy was complete because people were being drawn to Jesus. He concluded by expressing the true joy of a servant leader. He said:

He must increase, but I must decrease.
JOHN 3:30

John was full of joy because God was accomplishing His will right before his eyes! He knew his place was second chair to the One God had sent to bring salvation to all people. A servant leader's greatest joy comes when he or she sees God at work, and he or she is part of it. Servant leadership thrives on God-given passion for the success of God's plan.

Servant leaders find joy when God's will is done. They know they must become less and Christ must become greater. This attitude is consistent with servant leadership principles 1 and 2:

SERVANT LEADERSHIP PRINCIPLE 1
Servant leaders humble themselves and wait for God to exalt them.

SERVANT LEADERSHIP PRINCIPLE 2
Servant leaders follow Jesus rather than seek a position.

John's joy was different from Apollos's enthusiasm. Apollos had passion without knowing all the facts. John, on the other hand, had true joy because he saw God's plan for his life and for Jesus' honor being completed right before him.

Your Enthusiasm

Your God-given enthusiasm is sometimes your only source of joy in ministry. As you lead, you'll face obstacles and disappointments. People will criticize you. Sometimes they'll question your motives. But the sincere desire to know God's will and the passion God puts in your heart for His work absorb these negative reactions and allow you to move forward with your ministry. Just as mission is a source of endurance for a servant leader, vision is a source of passion. Seeing and working toward God's future for those you lead and serve stoke the fires of passion when others resist you.

What has God burned in your heart to do for the mission of God?
The one thing I do for God that makes my heart beat fast is ...

If I could do one thing for God, it would be to ...

SUMMARY

- Enthusiasm is a God-given desire to serve God by meeting the needs of others.
- Enthusiasm alone doesn't make you a servant leader.
- Your God-given enthusiasm is sometimes your only source of joy in ministry.
- Your enthusiasm is the beginning of a fruitful life in Christ.
- Servant leaders find joy when God's will is done. Servant leaders know they must become less and Christ must become greater.

Turn to the SERVE profile on the following page. Complete each section of the profile from the information you've gained from your study of weeks 2–3. Be prepared to share these insights with your group at the next session.

1. Will Mancini, *Church Unique: How Missional Leaders Cast Vision, Capture Culture, and Create Movement*, Kindle edition (Hoboken, NJ: Jossey-Bass, 2008), 834).
2. J. P. Louw and Eugene Albert Nida, *Greek-English Lexicon of the New Testament Based on Semantic Domains* (Swindon, England: United Bible Societies, 1988), 1:297, 8.

MY SERVE PROFILE

Believing that God has prepared me for servant leadership, I'm discovering that He's molded me in the following areas.

- God has given me these spiritual gifts (see week 2, day 3):

- God has allowed these experiences to guide me for His purposes (see week 2, day 5):

- God has created me to relate to others most naturally in this way (see week 3, day 1):

- God has given me opportunities to develop these vocational skills that can be used in His service (see week 3, day 4):

- God has burned in my heart the enthusiasm to serve in this area of ministry (see week 3, day 5):

I commit these gifts, talents, and abilities to God and His kingdom's service.

Signed _____ Date _____

Week 4

HOW TO EQUIP OTHERS

This Week's Memory Verse

He personally gave some to be apostles, some prophets, some evangelists, some pastors and teachers, for the training of the saints in the work of ministry, to build up the body of Christ.
EPHESIANS 4:11-12

Long before modern managers, Jesus was busy preparing people for the future. He was not aiming to pick out a crown prince, but to create a successor generation. ... When the time came for him to leave, he did not need to put in place a crash program of leadership development—the curriculum had been taught for three years in a living classroom.[1]
LEIGHTON FORD

I summited Mount Rainier in Washington State on my 60th birthday. It was my second attempt at the 14,410-foot peak. I had attempted it two years before only to turn back at the top of Disappointment Cleaver. On the second attempt I stood in the volcano crater at the top with five friends celebrating the accomplishment and 60 years of God's blessings. What was the difference between the two climbs? Experience and preparation. Both trips began with two days of mountaineering training, and having experienced the phenomenon of climbing in crampons on steep slopes and on loose rock, I was able to reach the goal with my guide and fellow climbers. If you're like me, you don't decide on Monday to climb Mount Rainier on Saturday. You need a guide, training, and experience to get to the top and back safe.

Servant leadership means recruiting people to climb the mountain of calling, but it also includes guiding and training them to fulfill that calling. To equip someone on mission with you is to answer the nagging question, How do I do this? We call men and women to trust and follow Jesus as we live out God's mission call on our lives. We cast vision and tell stories of transformed lives and communities. The Holy Spirit draws people to join you and those serving with you to join Him on mission, but they still wonder whether they can do what's needed to see what you've seen and to be used by God in significant ways. Servant leaders serve those on mission with them by equipping them to do what's needed to complete God's call in their lives.

A primary task of all church leaders is to train others so that together they can effectively meet the group's goals and needs. Jesus spent three years training His disciples for their lifelong ministries. Paul reminded the Christians in Ephesus that those whom God gifted to lead were to equip others for service (see Eph. 4:12). Leaders train and motivate others as they work together toward mutual goals in ministry.

Up to this point in the study, you've spent most of your time looking inwardly at your relationship with Christ and learning how to be a servant leader like Jesus. By now you've begun to understand Jesus' expectations of leaders and to discover ways He's prepared you to be a unique servant leader.

This week will introduce you to the importance of equipping others as part of your role as a servant leader. You'll discover five steps to equip others, you'll observe how Jesus equipped His closest followers, and you'll examine other biblical examples of leaders who trained others to carry out the mission of the church.

This week's study isn't exhaustive. It's only a starting place for effective leadership training in the church. The principles introduced here, however, are important for anyone who wants to follow the biblical precept to EQUIP others for service.

This Week You Will

- Understand the need to encourage others to serve in the body of Christ (day 1).
- Learn how to qualify persons you encourage to join you in service (day 2).
- Seek to understand the needs of those you equip for service (day 3).
- Discover areas in which you can instruct those you equip (day 4).
- Learn why prayer is your most powerful tool to lead and equip others (day 5).

Servant Leaders **EQUIP** *Others*

ENCOURAGE THEM TO SERVE.

QUALIFY THEM FOR SERVICE.

UNDERSTAND THEIR NEEDS.

INSTRUCT THEM.

PRAY FOR THEM.

1. Leighton Ford, *Transforming Leadership* (Downers Grove, IL: InterVarsity Press, 1993), 279.

Day 1
ENCOURAGE THEM TO SERVE

Today You Will
- Learn why you're responsible as a servant leader to EQUIP others for ministry.
- Observe ways Jesus encouraged His disciples in ministry.
- Observe the way Barnabas encouraged Paul to meet a need in Antioch.
- Identify people you can encourage to join you in ministry.

Servant Leaders **EQUIP** *Others*

☛ **ENCOURAGE THEM TO SERVE.**

QUALIFY THEM FOR SERVICE.

UNDERSTAND THEIR NEEDS.

INSTRUCT THEM.

PRAY FOR THEM.

The founding senior fellows of B. H. Carroll Theological Institute huddled around a conference table in a friend's office to confirm God's call in their lives: returning theological education to the local church through accessible, affordable, and achievable degrees. They resigned from the positions of teaching and administration in which they'd served to fully devote themselves to this adventure of faith. Once all the documents and goals were in place, they began the public, risky task of recruiting donors, faculty, and students.

High-fiving a shared dream is one thing. Encouraging others to join you is another. Servant leaders like Jesus serve those the Holy Spirit has called to join the mission of God by encouraging them to serve. Servant leaders know it's their responsibility to equip others for service. Ken Blanchard wrote:

One aspect of a job well done as a servant leader is how well we have prepared others to carry on after our season of leadership influence is completed. Our leadership legacy is not just limited to what we accomplished, but it includes what we leave behind in the hearts and minds of those with whom we had a chance to teach and work.[1]

Your job as a servant leader is to discover persons who are ready for service. You're also to equip other leaders to serve with you in ministry. The church functions best when—
1. members know how God has molded them for service;
2. members are equipped for the ministry they've been prepared to do.

Equipping others for service follows servant leadership principle 6:

SERVANT LEADERSHIP PRINCIPLE 6
Servant leaders share their responsibility and
authority with others to meet a greater need.

The First Step to EQUIP Others

Servant leaders encourage others to become involved in ministry. Because servant leaders know the joy of finding their place of service in the mission of God, they want others to share that joy. Servant leaders know that a person who's not involved in ministry is missing out on part of God's plan for his or her life.

EQUIP OTHERS FOR SERVICE, STEP 1
Encourage them to become involved in ministry.

To encourage literally means *to call to one's side.* You encourage others when you stand alongside them for a time to comfort and assist.

Jesus Encouraged His Disciples

Jesus called the twelve to follow Him to the cross and to be His witnesses throughout the world. He spent much of His time encouraging them. John 14 contains some of Jesus' most encouraging words to His followers. His disciples were concerned for themselves and their Master. The closer they came to Jerusalem, the more troubled they became about what would happen to them and to Him.

Read John 14:1-4. What encouragement did Jesus give His followers?

Read verses 5-7. Thomas asked the question that may have been on all their minds: "How can we know the way?" (v. 5). How did Jesus' response encourage His followers?

Read verses 12-14. What did Jesus promise His followers?

How do you think these promises encouraged them to join Jesus in ministry?

How do these promises encourage you to serve?

Jesus said He would send another Counselor to be with them forever (see v. 16). Another name for the Holy Spirit of God is Encourager.[2] Jesus said He wouldn't leave His disciples as orphans but would send His Holy Spirit to be with them. Knowing His followers would need His presence to guide and encourage them in the future, Jesus equipped them by encouraging them to count on His power as they served.

Barnabas Encouraged Paul

Read Acts 11:19-24. You met Barnabas in weeks 2–3. What were Barnabas's spiritual gifts (see week 2, day 3)?

What was his relational style (week 3, day 2)?

The church in Jerusalem heard about what was happening in Antioch, that the Lord's hand was on the church, and that "a large number who believed turned to the Lord" (v. 21). The church sent Barnabas to Antioch.

What does verse 23 say Barnabas did when he saw the evidence of the grace of God on the people?

The Bible states that Barnabas was "a good man, full of the Holy Spirit and of faith" (v. 24). God used him to bring many people to the Lord. Barnabas was an encouraging servant leader.

As the church in Antioch grew in number, a need arose for solid teaching about the ways of God and the promised Messiah. The new converts needed teaching that would ground them in their walk with the Lord. Barnabas recognized this need.

Read Acts 11:25-26. What did Barnabas do in response?

What did Barnabas and Saul do together?

Barnabas saw a need in the young church in Antioch. The many new converts needed strong, biblical teaching. Barnabas knew Saul of Tarsus was an experienced teacher of the Scriptures. Barnabas traveled to Tarsus and encouraged the Pharisee-turned-Christian to come with him and help meet a need by teaching new Christians. Barnabas met a need in the young church in Antioch by encouraging Saul to join him in a teaching ministry.

Read again verse 26. How long does the Bible say the two taught the people?

How do you think this ministry affected the church?

Barnabas was a servant leader who encouraged Saul to join him in ministry. This same Saul soon became the greatest missionary the church has ever known. Knowing the importance of encouragement, Paul told the Christians in Thessalonica on two different occasions to encourage one another:

> Encourage one another with these words.
> **1 THESSALONIANS 4:18**

> Encourage one another and build each other up as you are already doing.
> **1 THESSALONIANS 5:11**

The church has always had men and women like Barnabas. They never lead alone. They equip others by encouraging them to serve with them in ministry.

PERSONAL EVALUATION

Jesus modeled ways you can encourage others in ministry by reminding them of His power and presence in their lives. As you consider your role as a servant leader who can encourage others to take up a place of ministry, prayerfully answer the following questions.

What did Jesus say to His disciples that's most encouraging to you?

You may have had someone like Barnabas in your life. This person came to you and invited you to join him or her in a ministry that eventually led you to a place of service. If you've had such a person in your life, record that person's name. State what he or she asked you to do that propelled you into ministry.

You may be serving in a leadership position now. Write the names of one or two people you know whom you could encourage to join you in your ministry.

What do you see in them that makes you believe they're ready for service?

As you consider encouraging others to find a place of ministry, evaluate your own life. Is there anything in your life that would cause another person not to accept your invitation for service? Proverbs 27:19 states:

> The heart reflects the person.
> **PROVERBS 27:19**

What does your heart reflect to others? Think about that question for a moment and prayerfully record your answer.

SUMMARY

- Turn your attention to those you can equip for ministry.
- EQUIP others for service, step 1: Encourage him or her to become involved in ministry.
- Jesus modeled ways you can encourage others in ministry by reminding them of His power and presence in their lives.
- Barnabas met a need in the young church in Antioch by encouraging Saul to join him in a teaching ministry.
- Because servant leaders know the joy of finding their place of service in the mission of God, they want others to share that joy.

1. Ken Blanchard and Phil Hodges, *Lead like Jesus: Lessons from the Greatest Leadership Role Model of All Time,* Kindle edition (Nashville: Thomas Nelson, 2006), 59.
2. The King James Version reads "Comforter"; the NIV and HCSB, "Counselor"; and the NASB, "Helper." All three translations come from the same Greek word, which means "one who appears in another's behalf." William F. Arndt and Wilbur F. Gingrich, *A Greek-English Lexicon of the New Testament and Other Early Christian Literature* (Chicago: University of Chicago Press, 1957).

Day 2
QUALIFY THEM FOR SERVICE

Today You Will
- Learn step 2 to EQUIP others.
- Understand the meaning of *qualify* as applied to equipping others.
- Observe how Jesus qualified those who wanted to follow Him.
- Examine the way Paul taught Timothy to qualify others for ministry.
- Identify ways you can qualify those you've encouraged.

Servant Leaders **EQUIP** *Others*

ENCOURAGE THEM TO SERVE.

☞ QUALIFY THEM FOR SERVICE.

UNDERSTAND THEIR NEEDS.

INSTRUCT THEM.

PRAY FOR THEM.

The Second Step to EQUIP Others

To encourage someone to get involved in ministry isn't enough. Encouragement without training is like enthusiasm without direction: you move around a lot, but little gets done! Servant leaders guide and train those they encourage to join them in ministry. Jesus didn't say, "I will make you fish for people!" (Mark 1:17) and then leave Simon and Andrew to figure out things on their own. He invested the next three years of His life equipping them for what He'd called them to do. As a servant leader, you too must equip those you invite to serve with you. Let's look at the next step of how to EQUIP others.

EQUIP OTHERS FOR SERVICE, STEP 2
Qualify them for service.

In today's lesson *qualify* has two meanings:
1. The first meaning is to meet certain expectations for being a follower of Christ. These include the person's spiritual condition and a willingness to be a servant to others.
2. The second meaning is to know whether a person is competent for the ministry you've encouraged them to enter. This meaning relates to the person's SERVE profile (see week 3, day 5) and specific skills related to the ministry he or she has agreed to do.

Let's explore in more depth these meanings of being qualified for service.

1. A servant leader qualifies those he equips by holding them to biblical standards of discipleship and by testing their willingness to be servants to others. Jesus qualified those who followed Him by holding up high standards of discipleship. In Luke 14, after Jesus' story about voluntarily taking backseats, Luke stated, "Great crowds were traveling with Him" (v. 25). Most church leaders would see this as a good thing. Jesus, on the other hand, knew most of those people had no clue about what following Him actually meant.

> **Read Luke 14:26-27. What qualifications did Jesus give for following Him?**

> **Read verses 28-32. What was Jesus' point in providing these examples?**

> **Read verse 33. What was Jesus' final qualification for being one of His disciples?**

Jesus was very clear about the cost of discipleship. He risked losing large numbers in order to keep those who trusted Him and His mission. Jesus began equipping those who followed Him by holding up high standards of discipleship. As a leader who follows Jesus' example, you should make the cost of service to others very clear.

At the same time, keep in mind that no one is perfect. You can expect too much of people before they're mature in Christ. The danger of legalism exists anytime you hold someone to biblical standards for discipleship. No one lives up to the biblical ideal. Therefore, think of yourself as a minister …

> … not of the letter, but of the Spirit. For the
> letter kills, but the Spirit produces life.
> **2 CORINTHIANS 3:6**

The opposite danger of legalism, however, is to have no standards for those who serve in the church. Too many churches suffer because the people recruited to serve aren't biblically qualified to serve. To equip leaders effectively, seek a loving balance between biblical standards and the reality of human sinfulness.

Complete the following statement: The first meaning of *to qualify* is ...

2. A servant leader qualifies those he equips by knowing their skills and gifts for the ministry he's asked them to do. The leader must know whether a person is competent for a particular ministry. A leader must ask the question, *Does this person know how to do what I'm asking him to do?* The Bible provides a model for qualifying others for service in this sense.

Read 2 Timothy 2:2.

What you have heard from me in the presence of many witnesses, commit to faithful men who will be able to teach others also.
2 TIMOTHY 2:2

What did Paul tell Timothy to do?

The pattern of sharing Jesus' message, as outlined by Paul, was:

PAUL → TIMOTHY → RELIABLE MEN → OTHERS

As Timothy's mentor, Paul trained him as they traveled together (see Acts 16:1-5). When Paul felt Timothy was qualified to carry out ministry without him, the missionary left Timothy in Ephesus to lead the church (see 1 Tim. 1:3). Paul later wrote the young pastor and told him to entrust what he'd learned from him to faithful men who would also "be qualified to teach others" (2 Tim. 2:2, NIV). *Qualified* in this verse means *to be fit or competent for something.* Paul told Timothy to find "reliable" (NIV) or "faithful" (HCSB) men whom he could train to teach others. That pattern is still valid for equipping leaders today. A contemporary model of Paul's instructions would be:

How do you know whether people are qualified to carry out the task you've encouraged them to do?

1. Examine their SERVE profiles. If the church doesn't have these on file for every member, lead persons you're qualifying through this study and ask them to complete the SERVE profile. This will introduce them to Jesus' teachings on leadership and give them a greater understanding of how God has prepared them for ministry in the church.

2. Compare their SERVE profiles with the job description you, the ministry, or the church created for the position. Their spiritual gifts, experiences, vocational skills, and passion should match the ministry and needs you've encouraged them to become involved in.

3. Spend time with them to understand their heart and their desire to serve God.

Complete the following statement: The second meaning of *to qualify* is:

REVIEW

Complete the following statements as a review of today's study.

EQUIP others for service, step 2 is:

A servant leader qualifies those he equips by:

Another way a servant leader qualifies those he equips is by:

PERSONAL EVALUATION

Yesterday you prayerfully considered one or two people you could encourage to be involved in ministry. Today consider their qualifications to serve by answering the following questions.

Do you know they're growing disciples of Christ?
Name _____ Yes No   Name _____ Yes No

Do you know they're reliable and faithful people?
Name _____ Yes No   Name _____ Yes No

Do you know their SERVE profiles?
Name _____ Yes No   Name _____ Yes No

If you answered yes to the previous question, what does their SERVE profile tell you?

If you answered no, consider a time to lead them through this study.

What skills would you need to teach them before they'd be qualified to carry out what you asked them to do?

One goal of servant leadership is to equip others for ministry. One aspect of equipping others is qualifying them to serve. Jesus refused to let anyone follow Him without telling them the qualifications of discipleship. How can the church do anything less?

SUMMARY

- EQUIP others for service, step 2: Qualify them to serve.
- A servant leader qualifies those he equips by holding them to biblical standards of discipleship and by testing their willingness to be servants to others.
- When holding others to standards of holy living, seek a loving balance between biblical standards and the reality of human sinfulness.
- A servant leader qualifies those he equips by knowing their skills and gifts for the ministry he's asked them to do.
- One way to qualify a person is to know his or her SERVE profile.

Day 3
UNDERSTAND THEIR NEEDS

The reality is that most ministry training, whether the academic
kind that leads to a degree or the more practical kind based
in a church, is geared toward telling more than listening.[1]
STEVE OGNE AND TIM ROEHL

Today You Will
- Learn step 3 to EQUIP others.
- Observe ways Jesus understood the needs of His disciples.
- Learn two ways to understand the needs of those you equip.
- Evaluate your progress in equipping another person for ministry.

Servant Leaders **EQUIP** *Others*

ENCOURAGE THEM TO SERVE.

QUALIFY THEM FOR SERVICE.

☞ UNDERSTAND THEIR NEEDS.

INSTRUCT THEM.

PRAY FOR THEM.

Looking Back

Complete each word in the process of equipping others.

E _____ (see 1 Thess. 5:11)

Q _____ (see 2 Tim. 2:2)

As a servant leader, you encourage others to join you in ministry. You also qualify them for the service you've invited them to do. Today you'll learn the next step in equipping others for ministry.

The Third Step to EQUIP Others

In my world of theological education it's relatively easy to spot a need in a student's work. Misspelled words, run-on sentences, and illogical arguments stand out like a bad pitch in Major League Baseball. A teacher's temptation is simply to mark an answer wrong or give a grade without commenting on a paper, especially if you have a large class of students taking a required course for graduation. But if you want to be a servant leader to your learners, when you recognize a consistent inadequacy in their work, you take the time to discover the whys and whats of their misunderstanding. You invest in a conversation to understand their need and then make recommendations for ways they can improve. This approach may mean limiting your time in the faculty lounge so that you can tutor a potentially great student. Equipping others means observing and listening in order to understand the needs of those you lead and serve.

EQUIP OTHERS FOR SERVICE, STEP 3
Understand their needs and respond to them.

1. OBSERVE THEM AS THEY MINISTER. Jesus equipped His disciples by understanding their needs. Here's one example of how He did this. This encounter came after Jesus' transfiguration. As Jesus and His three closest followers approached a crowd of people, a man came to Jesus in the crowd.

Read Matthew 17:14-21.[2] What did the man ask Jesus?

What did the man say about Jesus' disciples?

How did Jesus reply when the disciples asked Him why they were unable to drive out the demon?

Jesus knew why His disciples were unable to heal the boy. He said they lacked faith and prayer in their lives. By observing the fruit of the disciples' ministry, Jesus understood their need to trust and pray more. Jesus equipped His disciples by observing their actions and by understanding their needs.

How does this apply to your role as someone who equips others for ministry? Jesus observed His disciples as they followed Him. One way to understand the needs of those you equip is to observe them as they participate in ministry. Observation will reveal what they need to become more effective servants.

Choose the statement(s) you believe to be the best way to observe a potential leader and to understand his or her need.

____ **Wait for the one you're equipping to come to you and ask for help.**
____ **Wait for someone to complain about how the person is doing his or her job.**
____ **Spend time with her while she carries out her ministry.**
____ **Ask others how the person is doing in his or her ministry.**

One way to understand a person's need is to observe him as he carries out ministry. To equip others means spending time with them in ministry so that you can observe their actions and understand their needs.

2. LISTEN TO THEIR REQUESTS. Another way to understand the needs of those you equip is to listen. The easiest way to discover a need is to ask, "How can I help you?" I promise that the person you're equipping will have an answer. But be prepared to respond with more than an answer like "Oh, I hear you." You'll need to be ready to truly help them after you've asked what their needs are.

Read Luke 11:1-4. What need did a disciple ask Jesus to address?

How did Jesus respond?

The disciples watched Jesus perform many powerful acts among the people. They also watched Jesus spend many hours in prayer. They sensed a need for spiritual power in their own lives. They wanted what they observed in their Master's life. Once as Jesus returned from a time of prayer, one of His disciples asked Him to teach them to pray. He responded to their need.

Jesus understood His follower's need because He listened to his request. He equipped the twelve for ministry by modeling prayer in front of them and by responding to their request when they asked Him about this habit in His life.

A second way to understand the needs of those you equip is to listen to their requests.

Record some of the most frequently asked questions by those you're equipping. If you aren't currently equipping someone, what questions do you think people may ask you?

You can understand needs simply by listening to the questions asked by those you recruit to serve.

REVIEW

Complete the following phrases to review today's lesson.

EQUIP others to serve, step 3 is:

One way to understand needs is:

Another way to understand the needs of those you equip is:

God has given you an opportunity to help build up the church by equipping others for works of service. This week be in prayer each day about whom you can invite to join you in ministry.

SUMMARY

- EQUIP others for service, step 3: Understand their needs.
- To equip others means spending time with them in ministry so that you can observe their actions and understand their needs.
- One way to understand the needs of those you equip is to observe them as they participate in ministry.
- Another way to understand the needs of those you equip is to listen.
- By this time you should have someone in mind whom you could invite to join you in ministry.

1. Steve Ogne and Tim Roehl, *TransforMissional Coaching: Empowering Leaders in a Changing Ministry World*, Kindle edition (Nashville: B&H Publishing, 2008), 123.
2. Some translations don't include verse 21. Check your Bible's margins or study notes for text and explanation.

Day 4
INSTRUCT THEM

A key activity of an effective servant leader is to act as a performance coach—making an ongoing investment into the lives of those who follow.[1]
KEN BLANCHARD

Today You Will
- Learn step 4 to EQUIP others.
- Observe ways Jesus instructed His followers.
- Discover the way Paul instructed young Timothy in ministry.
- Evaluate possible areas of instruction as you EQUIP others.

Servant Leaders **EQUIP** *Others*

ENCOURAGE THEM TO SERVE.

QUALIFY THEM FOR SERVICE.

UNDERSTAND THEIR NEEDS.

☛ **INSTRUCT THEM.**

PRAY FOR THEM.

Looking Back

Fill in each blank with the word the letter represents.

E _____ (see 1 Thess. 5:11)

Q _____ (see 2 Tim. 2:2)

U _____ (see Luke 11:1)

The Fourth Step to EQUIP Others

Leaders make a big mistake when they forget to instruct those they recruit. Too many times leaders invite others to become involved in ministry and then leave them alone to guess what they should do. Problems always arise when workers go untrained.

To orient our ministry directors to the work of the others, we dedicated a series of staff meetings to learning from a director what his or her ministry did each week. Our English-language director led us all up to the rooms where more than 150 internationals met each week to learn English. To give us a sense of what the students would experience on their first day of class, she handed out our registration forms, which were in Bulgarian. Her husband, who was from Bulgaria, spoke to us only in his native language, and we could use only Bulgarian to get our questions answered while filling out our forms. Needless to say, we got a good taste not only of the awkwardness the students must have felt but also of the director's patience and love for the students. To instruct someone isn't simply to pass on information. It requires putting that information in the context of people's lives.

EQUIP OTHERS FOR SERVICE, STEP 4
Instruct them.

Instructing is part of leading. Followers need to know what's expected of them and how to carry out the task assigned to them. Jesus equipped His followers by instructing them. Let's look at His example.

Jesus' Example

Jesus constantly taught His disciples. He trained them about the nature of the kingdom of God (see Matt. 13:1-52). He explained His mission (see Mark 10:32-34). He performed a miracle to teach a lesson (see Mark 4:35-41). Occasionally, He had to instruct His disciples on their attitude about being His followers.

Read Luke 17:7-10.

> Which one of you having a slave tending sheep or plowing will say
> to him when he comes in from the field, "Come at once and sit down
> to eat"? Instead, will he not tell him, "Prepare something for me to eat,
> get ready, and serve me while I eat and drink; later you can eat and
> drink"? Does he thank that slave because he did what was commanded?
> In the same way, when you have done all that you were commanded, you
> should say, "We are good-for-nothing slaves; we've only done our duty."
> **LUKE 17:7-10**

What was Jesus' point in this story?

**Review Jesus' teachings about being great and being first in Mark
10:35-45. How does the story in Luke 17:7-10 complement Jesus'
instruction to His disciples about being great in the kingdom of God?**

Jesus instructed His disciples to have the attitude of a servant. He taught that servants don't get special treatment when they do what's expected of them. This teaching supported His earlier messages about being great (see Mark 10:44) and humbling yourself (see Luke 14:11). This instruction also came before His act of washing the disciples' feet (see John 13). Jesus equipped His disciples for ministry by teaching them in a variety of ways and settings to have a servant's heart.

In the same way, servant leaders equip those who follow them by instructing them in a variety of ways on different occasions.

Paul Instructed Timothy

Paul, the leader who built a worldwide web of churches, also instructed those he recruited for ministry. The clearest example of this practice comes from his letters to Timothy.

Timothy joined Paul on his second missionary journey (Acts 16:1-3). Paul left him in Ephesus to lead the church there. Later Paul wrote to Timothy and explained to him how he wanted the young leader to serve those entrusted to his care.

Read 1 Timothy 4:11-16. Summarize Paul's instructions to Timothy.

Verse 11:

Verse 12:

Verse 13:

Verse 14:

Verse 15:

Verse 16:

Paul instructed Timothy to teach the things he'd outlined for him (see v. 11). He told the young man not to let others look down on him because he was young. Paul encouraged him to set an example in every area of his life for others to follow (see v. 12). Paul instructed the young pastor to devote himself to the public reading of Scripture, preaching, and teaching (see v. 13). Paul told him not to neglect his spiritual gift (see v. 14). The senior missionary taught Timothy to be diligent in these matters so that others could see his progress (see v. 15). Finally, Paul instructed Timothy to watch his life and doctrine closely, because others depended on him (see v. 16).

Paul equipped Timothy by teaching him how to minister to those in his care. Because his instructions were clear and specific, Timothy didn't have to wonder what his mentor expected of him. These instructions grew from Paul's experience and wisdom.

Servant leaders equip others by instructing them in the specifics of their ministry.

How Can You Instruct Others?

Let's assume for a moment that you've found a place of servant leadership with the Sunday-morning hospitality team. You've recruited your friend Steve to join you in this important ministry to guests. He agreed to serve with you but made it clear he knows nothing about a greeting ministry other than how to open a door, smile, and say, "Good morning!" Steve looks to you for instruction.

How would you instruct Steve about his attitude as a greeter?

What would you say to Steve about the importance of his ministry?

What are some specific details of this ministry you could teach him?

What are some resources that would help him become an effective greeter?

Although you may not be in a ministry of greeting guests, you can see how important instructions are to those you may recruit to help you. Servant leaders patiently instruct those they encourage to do ministry.

SUMMARY

- EQUIP others for service, step 4 is: Instruct them.
- Jesus instructed His followers in several ways and on different occasions about their attitudes as servant leaders.
- Servant leaders equip those who follow them by instructing them in a variety of ways on different occasions.
- Paul specifically taught Timothy the way he wanted the young pastor to minister in Ephesus.
- Servant leaders equip others by instructing them in the specifics of their ministry.

---

1. Ken Blanchard and Phil Hodges, *Lead like Jesus: Lessons from the Greatest Leadership Role Model of All Time,* Kindle edition (Nashville: Thomas Nelson, 2006), 164.

Day 5
PRAY FOR THEM

All the human energy of heart, mind, and will can achieve great human results, but praying in the Holy Spirit releases supernatural resources.[1]
J. OSWALD SANDERS

Today You Will
- Learn step 5 to EQUIP others.
- Observe ways Jesus prayed for those He called to serve.
- Discover the way Paul asked for prayer from those he appointed for service.
- Conclude your checklist to equip another person for ministry.

Servant Leaders **EQUIP** *Others*

ENCOURAGE THEM TO SERVE.

QUALIFY THEM FOR SERVICE.

UNDERSTAND THEIR NEEDS.

INSTRUCT THEM.

☛ PRAY FOR THEM.

Looking Back

Fill each blank with the word the letter represents.

E _____ (see 1 Thess. 5:11)
Q _____ (see 2 Tim. 2:2)
U _____ (see Luke 11:1)
I _____ (see 1 Tim. 4:11)

The four EQUIP actions you've studied so far this week can be done in human strength. You can encourage others under your own power. Your motivation to involve others can simply be because you need help! You can qualify others by your own efforts and standards. You can understand the needs of those you recruit by watching and listening to them. You can even instruct them in attitudes and specifics of their ministry based on human decisions. But one thing would be lacking in their lives: the power of God. Jesus observed a lack of power in His disciples when they couldn't cast out a demon:

> The disciples approached Jesus privately and said, "Why couldn't we drive it out?" "Because of your little faith," He told them. "For I assure you: If you have faith the size of a mustard seed, you will tell this mountain, 'Move from here to there,' and it will move. Nothing will be impossible for you. [However, this kind does not come out except by prayer and fasting.]"
> **MATTHEW 17:19-21**

Something was missing. This is why the final and most important step to EQUIP others for ministry is to pray for them.

The Fifth Step to EQUIP Others

We've seen that Jesus modeled every step of equipping others for ministry. He made this final step a priority in His ministry. In His final hours with those He loved, He prayed for them. Let's look at this special prayer.

Read John 17:6-19. Jesus prayed for His disciples' ministry.

- Jesus knew He'd taught them what they needed to know about His mission and about His Father: "the words that You gave Me, I have given them" (v. 8).
- Jesus prayed that they remain one in spirit and purpose: "Protect them by Your name … so that they may be one as We are one" (v. 11).
- Jesus prayed that they would have joy in their ministry: "I speak these things in the world so that they may have My joy completed in them" (v. 13).
- Jesus asked the Father to protect them from the Evil One: "I am not praying that You take them out of the world but that You protect them from the evil one" (v. 15).
- Jesus prayed that they be made holy by the truth of God's Word: "Sanctify them by the truth; Your word is truth" (v. 17).

Jesus equipped His disciples by praying for them.

EQUIP OTHERS FOR SERVICE, STEP 5
Pray for them.

Paul also prayed regularly for those he set aside for ministry (see Eph. 3:14-19; Phil. 1:3-6). Paul knew the power of prayer for all the saints as well as for himself. In Ephesians 6:11-17 he described the armor that equips believers for spiritual warfare. Read verses 18-20.

> Pray at all times in the Spirit with every prayer and request, and stay alert in this with all perseverance and intercession for all the saints. Pray also for me, that the message may be given to me when I open my mouth to make known with boldness the mystery of the gospel. For this I am an ambassador in chains. Pray that I might be bold enough in Him to speak as I should.
> **EPHESIANS 6:18-20**

Why did Paul conclude his teaching about spiritual conflict by talking about prayer?

What did Paul ask the Ephesians to pray for himself?

These verses are the conclusion to Paul's teaching about how God equips and protects those who follow Jesus. Paul taught that prayer is our most powerful weapon in waging spiritual battles. He asked the church to pray for all the saints on all occasions.

Knowing the power of prayer, Paul also asked for prayer for himself. He asked the Christians in Ephesus to pray for him while he ministered. He didn't ask them to pray that he would be released from prison, as most of us would. Instead, He asked for the words to witness boldly for Christ. He asked that he would receive the power and courage to speak fearlessly about the mystery of the gospel. Paul not only prayed for others but also asked others to pray for him.

Servant leaders pray for those they equip for ministry. They also ask for prayer so that they can lead boldly. Here we see the unique nature of Christian leadership. Leaders in the church know their power comes from God, not from themselves. They also know they're most effective when others support them in prayer. Church leaders are helpless without the prayers of others. These prayers may be all that keeps them standing in times of struggle and conflict.

No servant leader should stand to lead until he kneels to pray with those he serves. The power of equipping others isn't in technique but in prayer. Prayer should permeate every step to equip others. Prayer gives discernment, protection, and power to those who lead. Prayer is God's answer to our weakness as leaders.

SUMMARY

- EQUIP others for service, step 5 is: Pray for them.
- Jesus equipped His disciples by praying for them.
- Paul also prayed regularly for those he set aside for ministry.
- Servant leaders pray for those they equip for ministry. They also ask for prayer so that they can lead boldly.
- No servant leader should stand to lead until he kneels to pray with those he serves.
- Prayer is God's answer to our weakness as leaders.

REVIEW

Complete the following phrases to review this week's lessons.

EQUIP others for service, step 1 is:

EQUIP others for service, step 2 is:

EQUIP others for service, step 3 is:

EQUIP others for service, step 4 is:

EQUIP others for service, step 5 is:

MY EQUIP PROGRESS

Use the following statements to determine where you are in the process of equipping someone for ministry.

Name of the person I can encourage:

The ministry I have in mind:

Reasons he or she is qualified for this ministry:

His or her potential needs:

Potential areas of instruction:

Ways I can pray for him or her:

This week introduced you to an important aspect of servant leadership: EQUIP others for service. Next week you'll see the best way to multiply your effectiveness as a leader: through the power of TEAM ministry.

1. J. Oswald Sanders, *Spiritual Leadership: A Commitment to Excellence for Every Believer* (Chicago: Moody Press, 2007), 108.

Week 5
HOW TO SERVE IN TEAM MINISTRY

This Week's Memory Verse

He summoned the Twelve and began to send them out
in pairs and gave them authority over unclean spirits.
MARK 6:7

Job One for a leader is to assemble a leadership team, shape them
individually and collectively, and exercise leadership *through* that team.[1]
RALPH E. ENLOW JR.

When we observe Jesus' life and ministry, particularly the way He led the Kingdom movement of God, we see his choice of the twelve and his concentrated work with them. Why the twelve? Why not gather the masses to stand against the corrupt religious leaders or the Roman occupiers? Leighton Ford mused about how Jesus came to choose the team of twelve as part of his leadership on mission:

> The time had come to focus on a few. He could not handle all the needs; others must be trained. If the opposition could not be won over, it must be countered by having a loyal core who would carry on, regardless of what happened to him. He had to share the responsibility and ensure there was a succession of leadership. But he also had to be sure that those he chose were clear about the mission. Otherwise, the movement could dissipate through mistaken notions of what they were about.[2]

Jesus chose the twelve so that the mission of God, the mission of reconciliation, would continue when he returned to the Father.

Servant leaders team with others. They know effective leadership isn't a solo venture. Leadership is a team sport. Servant leaders know teams collectively move the ball down the field to reach their shared goal. Servant leaders know they're most effective when they can team with others who are equipped to meet a specific need.

Jesus' earthly ministry revolved around building a team of close followers. He called them, equipped them, and mobilized them for ministry. After Jesus had completed His mission on earth, these disciples would carry the message of God's salvation to the world. Jesus modeled team ministry for those He called to be servant leaders.

This week is about team ministry. You'll learn some basic principles about how teams work, and you'll be encouraged to begin forming a ministry team as part of your role as a servant leader.

This week concludes your study of *Jesus on Leadership*. Take time this week to look beyond this study to places where Christ wants you to serve. This study isn't the end of your understanding of servant leadership. It's only the beginning.

This Week You Will

- Understand why a servant leader leads best through ministry teams (day 1).
- Learn that teams work best when they work together (day 1).
- Examine how leaders empower those on their teams (day 2).
- Study the biblical principle of accountability (day 3).
- Learn that the best leaders are mentors to those on their teams (day 4).
- Learn the four next steps to becoming a servant leader and decide what you'll do to continue the process of becoming a servant leader (day 5).

Servant Leaders Serve in **TEAM** *Ministry*

TOGETHERNESS

EMPOWERMENT

ACCOUNTABILITY

MENTORING

1. Ralph E. Enlow Jr., *The Leader's Palette,* Kindle edition (Nashville: WestBow Press, 2013), 969.
2. Leighton Ford, *Transforming Leadership* (Downers Grove, IL: InterVarsity Press, 1991), 166.

Day 1
TOGETHERNESS

A unified and healthy leadership team
doesn't just happen. It has to be a priority.[1]
LARRY OSBORNE

Today You Will
- Define *team ministry.*
- Learn your role as a team leader.
- Observe ways Jesus modeled team ministry with His disciples.
- Learn the characteristics of working together as a team.
- Examine signs that a team is together.
- Evaluate your willingness to foster togetherness on a team.

Servant Leaders Serve in **TEAM** *Ministry*

☞ TOGETHERNESS

EMPOWERMENT

ACCOUNTABILITY

MENTORING

Leadership isn't a solo venture. It's a team sport. A leader is more like a player on a soccer team than like a pro golfer on tour. Leaders involve others to reach a shared goal. Team leaders are player-coaches. You'll never be an effective leader until you include those you lead. Leaders fail when they believe their efforts alone will achieve a group's goal.

The purpose of this study is for you to become a servant leader in team ministry. Servant leaders serve best when they serve with others. Although needs arise that demand the help of only one person, usually two or more people meet needs more effectively than an individual. You'll serve best as a leader when you team with others. Let's take a look at team ministry.

Jesus on Team Ministry

Jesus taught and modeled servant leadership (see week 1). He equipped His disciples for ministry (see week 4). Jesus also modeled team ministry. He seldom carried out ministry by Himself even though He was the Master and needed no one else to help meet needs. Yet no matter what He was doing, Jesus ministered with His disciples nearby. He usually had at least three disciples with Him wherever He went. By constantly having His closest followers near Him, He showed that the best lessons came from the classroom of experience. Jesus didn't need a ministry team, but He built one to ensure that ministry would continue when He returned to the Father.

Matthew, Mark, and Luke record the way Jesus commissioned His followers to do ministry in His name. Matthew 10 is a disciple's manual for ministry. Mark records that Jesus sent His disciples out two by two (see 6:7). He knew the advantage of two serving together as a team rather than one trying to meet needs alone.

Jesus modeled team ministry, and His disciples followed that example. When the Holy Spirit directed the church in Antioch to send members out to share the gospel with the Gentiles, God's Spirit told the church to select two members. After prayer and fasting, the church sent out Barnabas and Saul (see Acts 13:1-3). Ministry teams are the method the early church used to meet the need of evangelism. Ministry teams are the method the church of the 21st century will continue to meet needs effectively.

List examples of ministry teams in your church.

Why TEAM?

A team is a group of people bound together by a commitment to reach a shared goal. A team can be a group of college students playing intramural football, a group of researchers seeking the cure for a disease, or a group of Sunday School workers teaching the Bible to a roomful of four-year-olds. A team can put a space probe on Mars or feed the poor.

The business world recognizes the power of teams. The Harvard Business School says a team is a small number of people with complementary skills who are committed to a common purpose, performance goals, and approach for which they hold themselves mutually accountable.[2] So how do teams apply to servant leadership and the church?

We've spent four weeks studying servant leadership and the importance of meeting needs. Servant leadership begins when a disciple takes the role of a servant to meet a need. Servant leadership is also about setting self aside so that Christ can be Lord.

Write your own definition of *servant leadership*.

Team ministry affords servant leaders a way to multiply their callings to meet the needs of others. Multiplying ministry is consistent with servant leadership principle 7:

SERVANT LEADERSHIP PRINCIPLE 7
Servant leaders multiply their leadership by empowering others to lead.

For the purposes of this study, I describe team ministry this way:

TEAM MINISTRY
A group of disciples bound together under the lordship
of Christ who are committed to the shared goal
of meeting a particular need related to the mission

Team ministry is the method servant leaders generally use to carry out the work of ministry. This week you'll discover four characteristics of team ministry: togetherness, empowerment, accountability, and mentoring.

Team Ministry Begins When You're Together with Others

Team ministry occurs where there's a sense of being part of a team. The first characteristic of a team is the sense that we're in this together. Team members sense that each person belongs and that the other team members respect one another. Team ministry starts when those on the team sense they're together for a reason greater than themselves, and that reason is the mission of God and their participation in it.

TEAM CHARACTERISTIC 1
Togetherness

Teams form to reach a common goal or meet a need related to the mission. Like a food-pantry team or an after-school tutoring team, teams form to carry out a specific function. Evangelism teams form to reach the goal of introducing others to Christ. Worship teams form to lead churches to the throne of God more effectively. Teams have a purpose for forming that contributes to the accomplishment of their shared mission. That purpose drives them throughout their existence. When they've reached their goal or met the need, the team disbands or redirects its energy to other goals. The team celebrates its performance, and its members may or may not reform into a new team.

Unity is a key to a team's success.

Read Matthew 12:30. What were two options for being on Jesus' team?

Jesus insisted that those who follow Him share His values and purposes. The disciples either agreed with who He was and what He did, or they worked against Him. Jesus even scolded Peter for not supporting the Master's clear purpose for ministry (see 16:23).

Team members have a deep sense that they share a common and an important reason for being together. This gives the team a sense of togetherness. This sense of unity and purpose is the glue that holds the team together until it has reached its goal. Division in a team can be deadly to its existence. Pastor Larry Osborne warns that disunity is a sin that hinders the work of the Holy Spirit in ministry teams. He concludes:

> That's why maintaining unity is so important. It not only impacts organizational health; it impacts spiritual health and power.[3]

When Teams Are Together

We've already noted that the first characteristic of an effective team is a sense that we're in this together.

What are some signs that a team is together?

We've seen that Jesus insisted on unity in His ministry team of disciples. Another sign of togetherness is that He shared authority and responsibility with those on His team. As the team's leader, Jesus modeled shared leadership. He invited His followers to do what He did with His same power and authority. This instilled confidence among His followers.

Read Mark 6:6-13. What two actions did Jesus take when He sent out His disciples as ministry teams (see v. 7)?

What other instructions did Jesus give His followers in verses 8-11?

What were the results of the twelve's mission (Mark 6:12-13)?

When Jesus sent out His twelve closest followers, He sent them out in teams of two. Jesus knew this proverb:

> Two are better than one because they have a good reward for their efforts. For if either falls, his companion can lift him up; but pity the one who falls without another to lift him up. Also, if two lie down together, they can keep warm; but how can one person alone keep warm? And if someone overpowers one person, two can resist him. A cord of three strands is not easily broken.
> **ECCLESIASTES 4:9-12**

Some have called this principle "the wisdom of two."

Jesus shared with the disciples His authority over the evil ones they would encounter (see Mark 6:7). He instructed them to take nothing except a staff for their journey (see v. 8). They were to take no extra clothing (see v. 9). When they entered a town, they were to stay in the same home for the duration of their visit (see v. 10). If someone didn't welcome them, they were to shake the dust off their feet as a sign of their displeasure (see v. 11). When the teams of two went out and preached the gospel (see v. 12), they experienced success in their mission (see v. 13). Jesus shared His leadership with the teams by sending and empowering them to carry out what He'd commissioned them to do.

Servant leaders in team ministry must maintain a balance between doing things themselves and encouraging others to participate. Although he or she may appear to have a servant attitude, a person who does the team's work alone isn't a genuine servant leader. Katzenbach and Smith give good conventional wisdom on this matter:

> Team leaders genuinely believe that they do not have all the answers— so they do not insist on providing them. They believe they do not need to make all key decisions—so they do not do so. They believe they cannot succeed without the combined contributions of all the other members of the team to a common end—and so they avoid any action that might constrain inputs or intimidate anyone on the team. Ego is not their predominant concern.[4]

Jesus fostered a sense of togetherness by sending out His disciples in twos rather than alone. He also shared leadership with His disciples. These actions gave them a sense of being part of His team to spread the gospel.

PERSONAL EVALUATION

Begin praying today about people you can lead to become a ministry team. Begin building a potential team by making a list of people who share your passion for a certain ministry need. Record their names.

What could you do for the Kingdom if you had six or eight other disciples who shared your heart for ministry?

Team ministry is about Christian servants who are committed to meeting needs. Jesus and His disciples modeled team ministry for us. You can model it for the rest of the church. Prayerfully consider how God can use you in team ministry.

SUMMARY

- Team ministry involves a group of disciples bound together under the lordship of Christ who are committed to the shared goal of meeting a particular need related to the mission.
- Jesus sent out His followers in ministry teams rather than one by one.
- As a servant leader, you're willing to share leadership with those who team with you to carry out ministry.
- TEAM characteristic 1 is togetherness, a sense that we're in this together. Unity is a key to effectiveness.
- As His team's leader, Jesus modeled shared leadership. He invited His followers to do what He did with the same power and authority.
- A team is together when its leader shares leadership and authority with the team.
- Servant leaders in team ministry must maintain a balance between doing things themselves and encouraging others to participate.

1. Larry Osborne, *Sticky Teams: Keeping Your Leadership Team and Staff on the Same Page,* Kindle edition (Grand Rapids, MI: Zondervan, 2010), 24.
2. Jon R. Katzenbach and Douglas K. Smith, *The Wisdom of Teams: Creating the High-Performance Organization* (Boston: Harvard Business School Press, 1993), 45.
3. Osborne, *Sticky Teams,* 27.
4. Katzenbach and Smith, *The Wisdom,* 131.

Day 2
EMPOWERMENT

People will support leaders who help them discover
who they are created to be and then empower them
to employ their talents, energies, and passions.[1]
REGGIE MCNEAL

Today You Will
- Learn how effective team leaders empower team members.
- Observe ways Jesus empowered His disciples.
- Discover the way Paul empowered Aquila and Priscilla.
- Identify ways you can empower others in team ministry.

Servant Leaders Serve in **TEAM** *Ministry*

TOGETHERNESS

☛ EMPOWERMENT

ACCOUNTABILITY

MENTORING

Write servant leadership principle 7 (see week 1, day 4).

Servant leaders in team ministry empower those on their teams to reach a shared goal. Members of a team must feel they're part of the team and empowered by their leader, or the team won't do its best work. If team members aren't empowered, the leader does all the work—and that's not a team. Calvin Miller clearly described this truth when he wrote:

Often a company or a church consists of a few hassled, harried leaders and a great many take-it-easy followers. ... Followers must be made to believe they are part of a team. They must be made to participate with the leader in the work the team has to do. Such participation will level out both the busyness at the top and the lackadaisical attitude at the bottom.[2]

A key word in Miller's thought is *participate*. Participation means team members are involved and feel they're contributing to the team's goal. Empowerment is about giving team members authority and resources to do their part of the work.

Every Member Is Important

Team ministry means every member has a place on the team. Each one can make a contribution toward the group's goal. Different spiritual gifts, experiences, relational styles, vocational skills, and enthusiasm make a ministry team complete. Teams demand different skills and gifts. Peter Drucker has noted:

> A common mistake is to believe that because individuals are all on the same team, they all think alike and act alike. Not so. The purpose of a team is to make the strengths of each person effective, and his or her weaknesses irrelevant.[3]

Putting a team together means finding people who share a common goal with you but who may be different from the ways you think or act. Team ministry reinforces the biblical teaching that the church has many parts but one body.

Review 1 Corinthians 12:14-26, which you studied in week 2, day 2, and identify two harmful thoughts that could destroy the church.

Paul warned each member of the church against two extremely harmful attitudes:
1. I don't belong and have nothing to contribute to the church.
2. I'm totally self-sufficient and don't need the other members of the body of Christ.

The Bible teaches that every member belongs and that every part needs all the others. Team ministry affirms this principle. Every member has a place of service in the church. Servant leaders who build ministry teams must help every member find a place of service. "I don't belong" and "I don't need you" are thoughts that undermine the unity of the body.

Jesus Empowered His Disciples

The mission of every New Testament church is to make disciples. You don't have to put a task force together to discover this mission. Jesus commissioned the twelve to make disciples: to turn lost, secular people into maturing disciples of Christ (see Matt 28:19-20). Every church should be working to carry out this mission that Christ gave it. But how were the disciples then and disciples now to find the power to do this mission?

Before Jesus assigned His disciples the Great Commission and ascended into heaven, He said:

> All authority has been given to Me in heaven and on earth.
> **MATTHEW 28:18**

Based on this truth, Jesus sent out His followers to make disciples. Jesus empowered His disciples by sharing His authority with them. You saw in Exodus 18 that Moses empowered his leaders with authority to make decisions among the people of Israel (see week 1, day 4). Yesterday you saw that Jesus sent His disciples out two by two and gave them His authority over the evil spirits they would encounter (see Mark 6:7).

TEAM CHARACTERISTIC 2
Empowerment

Read Acts 1:8.

> You will receive power when the Holy Spirit has come
> on you, and you will be My witnesses in Jerusalem,
> in all Judea and Samaria, and to the ends of the earth.
> **ACTS 1:8**

What did Jesus tell the disciples they would receive, and what would they become as a result?

Read Ephesians 1:18-21. What demonstration of God's power did Paul cite as evidence of the power that works in believers' lives?

Jesus promised His followers they would receive power to do their mission "when the Holy Spirit has come on you" (Acts 1:8). They would then become witnesses of the resurrection power in their lives as they sought to carry out the Great Commission. Jesus empowered His disciples to become witnesses by giving them the power of the Holy Spirit. He gave His mission team the power it needed to evangelize the world. Jesus enabled His disciples to reach the goal by giving them authority and power—the same power that raised Jesus from the dead (see Eph. 1:20). With these resources the disciples were able to make the right decisions and act with authority to carry out the mission of God.

What two things did Jesus give His disciples to empower them to carry out His mission?

As a servant leader, make sure your team members understand that they have access to the same resources for reaching the goals that God has assigned your team.

Paul Empowered His Workers

You don't empower people with a memo. Empowerment doesn't happen with the stroke of a pen or a keyboard. You empower people in real time. It takes time and effort to empower someone to do the work of a team member. Paul did this with many on his ministry team by living with them and by giving them responsibilities of service.

Read Acts 18:1-4. Whom did Paul meet and begin ministering with when he came to Corinth? What vocational skill did they share?

What did Paul do with Aquila and Priscilla?

Paul met a couple from Rome when he came to Corinth. Like himself, they were tent makers. Luke tells us Paul "stayed with them and worked" (v. 3). While on mission, Paul joined this Christian couple to work toward the goal of telling all people about Christ.[4] Verse 18 reveals that they went along with Paul as he traveled to his next mission point.

Paul stayed in Corinth for a year and six months (see v. 11). What do you think happened during this time that made Aquila and Priscilla want to travel with him?

A year and a half after his arrival in Corinth, Paul moved on in his journey of world evangelization. Luke tells us that Priscilla and Aquila were part of Paul's ministry team when he left Corinth. We don't know what happened to make them want to go, but Paul possibly recruited and trained them to do the work of missions. They also may have wanted to support Paul with their tent making so that he could minister full-time. Team ministry means all members contribute to the shared goal in their own ways.

Read Acts 18:19-21. What did Paul do with Priscilla and Aquila?

Why do you think he did this?

When Paul arrived in Ephesus, he realized the need for mature believers who could help the growing church there. He left Priscilla and Aquila in Ephesus to help lead the church. Paul equipped and empowered his two friends to become servant leaders. He left them in Ephesus because he knew they were trained to do the ministry they'd been called to do. They were servant leaders who desired to meet a need in the Ephesian church. This is also evidenced by their response to Apollos when he arrived in Ephesus (see vv. 24-26). They felt free to address a need in the young teacher's ministry.

How did Paul empower Priscilla and Aquila?

- He taught and modeled the gospel as he lived and worked with them. They apparently became part of his ministry team in Corinth.
- He invited them to join his ministry team as it traveled to the next mission point.
- He left them in Ephesus to create their own ministry team as he continued his journey.

To follow Paul's pattern of empowerment, you must—

- teach and model the gospel as you live and work with other believers;
- invite others to join you on your ministry team when you see they can contribute to the goal of your mission;
- empower them to take on ministry by themselves and form their own ministry teams.

Jesus modeled the *what* of empowerment. You empower your team with authority and power to reach your goal. Like Jesus, you empower with the authority of God's name and the power of His presence through the Holy Spirit.

Paul modeled the *how* of empowerment. You empower your team by living and working with them and inviting them to take on more responsibility along the way. Like Paul, you invest in the lives of those on mission with you in order to develop the values, skills, and ministry to live out their unique contributions to the mission of God.

PERSONAL EVALUATION

List ways you can empower your team members by sharing with them the resources of authority and power.

What authority do you have to share with them?

What resources can you share with them to aid them in their work?

What are some ways you can empower your team members?

How can you live and work with them?

End today's study by claiming God's authority and power in your life and praying for the wisdom to empower those on your ministry team.

SUMMARY

- Team ministry means every member has a place on the team, and each one can make a contribution toward the goal.
- TEAM characteristic 2 is empowerment. Servant leaders in team ministry empower members to reach a shared goal.
- Empowerment means giving members authority and resources to do their part.
- Jesus modeled the *what* of empowerment. You empower your team with authority and power to reach their goal.
- Paul modeled the *how* of empowerment. You empower your team by living and working with them and inviting them to take on more responsibility.

1. Reggie McNeal, *A Work of Heart: Understanding How God Shapes Spiritual Leaders,* Kindle edition (Hoboken, NJ: Jossey-Bass, 2000), 1257.
2. Calvin Miller, *The Empowered Leader: 10 Keys to Servant Leadership* (Nashville: B&H Publishing, 1995), 158.
3. Quotation from *Managing the Nonprofit Organization* by Peter F. Drucker. Copyright © 1990 by Peter F. Drucker. Reprinted by permission of HarperCollins Publishers Inc., 152–53.
4. Scholars argue about whether Aquila and Priscilla were believers before or after they met Paul. What's important is that we know by Acts 18:18 they were followers of Christ and coworkers with Paul.

Day 3
ACCOUNTABILITY

God demands accountability from us, His servant leaders. We must give an account of what we have done with what He has given to us—including the honored role of being leaders in His kingdom.[1]
TED ENGSTROM AND PAUL CEDAR

Today You Will
- Examine the biblical principle of accountability.
- Learn why effective team leaders are accountable for those on the team.
- Observe ways Jesus held His disciples accountable to His goals.
- Understand the importance of accountability among team members.

Servant Leaders Serve in **TEAM** Ministry

TOGETHERNESS

EMPOWERMENT

☞ ACCOUNTABILITY

MENTORING

Accountability makes team ministry possible. It's the ability to account for who team members are and what they've done. It's the glue that keeps team members together and working toward the same goal. With it team members can count on others to do what they say they'll do. Without it members decide on their own when, how, and whether they'll do their part of the work. Trust in others on the team and commitment to the same goal are elements of accountability in team ministry.

TEAM CHARACTERISTIC 3
Accountability

Jesus on Accountability

Jesus taught that all people will give an account to a holy God for their words and deeds. When a group of religious leaders accused Jesus of working for Satan, He responded:

> I tell you that on the day of judgment people will have
> to account for every careless word they speak.
> **MATTHEW 12:36**

Servant leaders humbly make themselves accountable to God through authentic friendships with other servant leaders like Jesus. If the leader isn't accountable in this highest sense, the team will never embrace this value.

Paul reminded the Roman Christians:

> Each of us will give an account of himself to God.
> **ROMANS 14:12**

Peter encouraged his readers not to worry if pagans didn't understand their lifestyle. They too …

> … will have to give account to him who is ready
> to judge the living and the dead.
> **1 PETER 4:5**

Accountability to God means giving an account for your behavior while on earth. It means telling the truth to the person to whom you're responsible for what you've done and said.

**If you had to give an account to God today for what you've done
and said, would it be acceptable to God?   Yes   No   Why?**

The Bible teaches that accountability is a component of your relationship with God. This sense of giving an account to God should affect the way you live your life. You'll find it hard to be accountable to people if you don't accept that you're accountable to God.

Mutual accountability refers to being responsible for what you say and do to persons you commit yourself to. An example is marriage. A couple promises to be faithful to each other. They're then responsible to each other to carry out that promise. Accountability in marriage keeps the couple together by building trust and displaying commitment.

If you're married, list two or three promises you made to your spouse for which you're accountable. If you aren't married, list some promises you're responsible to others to keep.

Teams work best when their members are accountable to one another for what they've agreed to be and do for the team. Accountability applies to every member of the team, including the leader.

Leaders Are Accountable for Their Group

Read Hebrews 13:17 and underline the reasons the writer asked members of the church to obey their leaders.

> Obey your leaders and submit to them, for they keep watch over your souls as those who will give an account, so that they can do this with joy and not with grief, for that would be unprofitable for you.
> **HEBREWS 13:17**

The writer to the Hebrews insisted that members of the church obey their leaders. He gave two reasons for this command:
1. The leaders are accountable for those in the church.
2. Their work will be a joy instead of a burden if the members follow.

This verse teaches that leaders are accountable for those under their care. Likewise, servant leaders are accountable for their team members as they work together to reach their shared goal. This verse also teaches that members should follow their leaders. Members are responsible to follow the leader's guidance. Trust in the leader and commitment to the church's mission cement the relationship between church leader and follower. The result is a joyful leader, and a joyful leader is an advantage for those on the team. If the leader is free to guide, he or she is free to move the group in the direction of the shared goal.

Leaders Are Accountable for the Goal

Servant leaders are accountable to keep the team focused on its goal for the mission. Jesus modeled this accountability for those in the school of servant leadership as He taught His disciples the true nature of His mission.

Read Mark 8:27-33. What did Peter's confession suggest about His belief in Jesus?

What did Peter's rebuke of Jesus indicate about his understanding of Jesus' identity?

How did Jesus hold Peter accountable for the truth about His identity?

Peter initially confessed that Jesus is the Messiah. He committed himself to Jesus' goal of carrying out God's plan of redemption. Yet he was unwilling to accept Jesus' words about His suffering and death. He pulled Jesus aside and rebuked Him. Peter trusted his concept of the Christ rather than what Jesus had taught. Peter's ideas threatened the mission of the Messiah and the unity of the disciples.

Jesus knew the danger of Peter's attitude. The team of disciples had to be unified on who Jesus was and the nature of His mission. Jesus confronted Peter's words by saying, "Get behind Me, Satan!" Jesus called Peter Satan because the disciple offered the same easy path to victory that Satan had posed to Jesus in the wilderness (see Luke 4:9-12). Jesus knew the Messiah must suffer and die to complete the Father's mission of redemption. Jesus was accountable to the Father to complete His mission as the Suffering Servant Messiah. As a leader, He knew the need for His followers to stay committed to the same goal He came to accomplish.

Accountability Among the Team Members

"No group ever becomes a team until it can hold itself accountable as a team."[2] No baseball team can get to the World Series until every team member makes himself accountable to the others to reach this goal. No Bible-study team will be what it says it wants to become unless all members are openly accountable to the team for their actions and words. Team members make themselves responsible to one another to do their part in reaching the shared goal. When you make yourself responsible to others on a ministry team, you become accountable to them. Team ministry means making yourself accountable to the other team members to reach your shared goal.

Team accountability can start when each member has a servant leader's heart.

Record servant leadership principle 3.

Jesus taught that greatness among His followers begins with being a servant to others. Being first starts with giving up personal rights to meet the needs of others:

> Whoever wants to become great among you must be your servant,
> and whoever wants to be first among you must be a slave to all.
> **MARK 10:43-44**

Team accountability happens when team members become servants to the goal of ministry and slaves to those on the team to help them reach that goal.

Jesus called His disciples to follow Him. They became leaders only after Jesus trained them and empowered them with His Holy Spirit. Servant leadership principle 2 states:

SERVANT LEADERSHIP PRINCIPLE 2
Servant leaders follow Jesus rather than seek a position.

You've seen that Jesus gave up His position in heaven to bring salvation to the world (see Phil. 2:5-11) and that He led from a servant's position. Jesus is your example of a servant leader who gave up position to meet the needs of others. Servant leaders share leadership with others to reach a common goal. Robert Greenleaf mused that the church of the future will have leaders who are willing to practice "followership." He wrote:

> Leadership in such an institution will be a different thing from what we customarily assume. ... It will be a role from which oversight is given to a much more fluid arrangement in which leaders and followers change places as many-faceted missions are undertaken and move into phases that call for different deployments of talent.[3]

Servant leaders know how to follow. Each person's first steps as a leader began as a follower. Disciples are learners who fall in line behind their Master. Because servant leaders know how to follow, they willingly allow others to lead when someone with a different SERVE profile fits the need better than their own. Servant leaders share leadership with others when the need dictates. This willingness to share leadership is an important aspect of accountability to God and to the team.

PERSONAL EVALUATION

Complete the following statements.

The concept of accountability is hard for me to accept because …

I experienced a sense of accountability to others when I …

If you're a ministry-team leader, record the goal to which you ask your team to be accountable.

List ways you can build trust and commitment among your team members to help them become accountable to one another.

SUMMARY

- TEAM characteristic 3 is accountability. Accountability makes team ministry possible.
- Trust of others on the team and commitment to the same goal are elements of accountability in team ministry.
- Jesus taught that all people will give an account to a holy God for their words and deeds.
- *Mutual accountability* refers to being responsible for what you say and do to persons you commit yourself to.
- Servant leaders are accountable to keep the team focused on its goal for the mission.
- Team ministry means making yourself accountable to the other team members to reach your shared goal.

1. Theodore Wilhelm Engstrom and Paul A. Cedar, *Compassionate Leadership*, Kindle edition (Ventura, CA: Regal Books, 2006), 641.
2. Jon R. Katzenbach and Douglas K. Smith, *The Wisdom of Teams: Creating the High-Performance Organization* (Boston: Harvard Business School Press, 1993), 60.
3. Robert K. Greenleaf, *Servant Leadership* (Mahwah, NJ: Paulist Press, 1977), 244.

Day 4
MENTORING

Behind everything you do should be the goal of developing
servant leaders who can take over when you leave.[1]
TED ENGSTROM AND PAUL CEDAR

Today You Will
- Examine the practice of mentoring.
- Observe ways Jesus mentored His disciples.
- Discover the way Paul instructed Timothy to be a mentor.
- Consider your need for a mentor.

Servant Leaders Serve in **TEAM** Ministry

TOGETHERNESS

EMPOWERMENT

ACCOUNTABILITY

☛ MENTORING

A mentor is a guide. Mentors lead others through new terrain because they've been there before and are equipped to lead. Mentors model what they want their followers to do. Their actions weigh as heavy as their words. Leaders in team ministry guide where the team is going and model the Christian lifestyle they want team members to follow.

We had pastoral interns on the staff where I pastored. I considered them part of my ministry team. Our pastoral interns did everything from opening the buildings on Sunday mornings to preaching in my absence. They had other duties too. One of them led our new-member-assimilation process. Another managed our church database. One led our men's ministry, and the fourth was a small-group leader. Each pastoral intern was in at least one place of servant leadership, and I had the privilege of guiding them. I knew what it was like to be in seminary while wanting to serve full-time. I knew what it was like to be certain you could do the job, but no one asked you to do anything. I also knew what it was like to know God had called you to a certain place of ministry, but you didn't seem to be there yet. I knew these things because I was a pastoral intern while I was in seminary, and someone who'd been where I was going made the effort to show me the way.

As a mentor, I guided our interns through their seminary days and modeled for them how I believe ministry is done. They were accountable to me for then way they carried out their assignments, and I pledged to guide them the best way I could.

TEAM CHARACTERISTIC 4
Mentoring

Servant leaders are mentors to people who are working with them in team ministry. Mentoring is the way Christ's work is passed on to the next generation of servant leaders. To mentor is to multiply Christ and Kingdom ministry in the life of another person.

Fill in these blanks. A mentor is a _____.

Leaders in team ministry _____ where the team is going and _____ the Christian lifestyle they want team members to follow.

Jesus on Mentoring

Jesus guided His disciples and modeled for them the way they should live as His followers. When Jesus called His disciples to follow Him, He meant for them to follow His example as well as His feet.

Read the following passages and record ways Jesus mentored His disciples.

How Jesus Mentored His Disciples

Matthew 5:1-2

Mark 6:32-44

Luke 6:12

John 13:3-5

Jesus mentored His disciples by teaching them. Matthew 5–7 records Jesus' Sermon on the Mount, Jesus' teachings about how Kingdom people live. Earlier in this study you read a passage showing that Jesus taught His disciples about leadership (see Mark 10:35-45).

Jesus also mentored His followers by demonstrating God's power in their lives. When the disciples thought there was no way to feed a crowd that had followed them all day, Jesus asked His Father to provide enough food from five loaves and two fish to feed the five thousand (see 6:32-44).

Jesus modeled a life of prayer for His followers. Luke 6:12 records that He prayed all night before choosing the twelve. In addition, we've already seen that Jesus equipped His followers when they asked Him to teach them to pray (see 11:1-4).

Jesus also modeled servant leadership for His disciples when He washed their feet (see John 13:3-5).

Fill in these blanks. Jesus mentored His disciples by _____ them and by _____ what He wanted them to do.

Paul on Mentoring

Paul was also a mentor. The apostle trained leaders in every church he started. This is one reason he was able to establish as many churches as he did.

You've already learned that mentoring means modeling actions you want your team members to follow. Paul urged believers in the Corinthian church to do just that.

Read 1 Corinthians 4:16.

I urge you to imitate me.
1 CORINTHIANS 4:16

Why did Paul instruct the Corinthians to imitate him?

Paul wrote, "I urge you to imitate me." The apostle wanted those who trusted his witness of Christ as Savior also to trust him in the way they lived their lives. We get our English word *mimic* from the Greek word translated *imitate*. As a mentor of leaders, Paul could say, "Mimic what I do."

Paul continued in the next verse:

> This is why I have sent Timothy to you. He is my dearly loved
> and faithful son in the Lord. He will remind you about my ways
> in Christ Jesus, just as I teach everywhere in every church.
> **1 CORINTHIANS 4:17**

Paul said Timothy would "remind you about my ways in Christ Jesus." When Paul couldn't personally model how he wanted the people to live, he sent an equipped follower. Timothy was someone he'd mentored in the faith.

Paul was Timothy's mentor. The more mature missionary taught Timothy to be a follower of Christ. Paul also taught him to be a servant leader.

Read 1 Timothy 4:12.

> Let no one despise your youth; instead, you should be an example
> to the believers in speech, in conduct, in love, in faith, in purity.
> **1 TIMOTHY 4:12**

What did Paul tell Timothy to do for the believers in the church?

In what areas of his life did Paul ask Timothy to demonstrate Christ?

Paul told Timothy to be an example for the believers in the church. We get our English word *type* from the Greek word translated *example* in this verse. Paul wanted the members of the church to see in Timothy the type of disciple they should be.

Timothy was to model for the church what a life in Christ looked like in the areas of speech, daily living, love, faith, and purity. He was to mentor others by modeling the behavior he wanted to see in their lives. How did Timothy know what these things looked like? Paul had mentored him. Mentoring means taking what you've caught from your mentor and sharing it with another person.

Servant leaders in team ministry model the ways they want team members to believe and act. Servant leaders model for others what Christ modeled for them.

In Need of a Mentor

Explaining the second promise of a Promise Keeper, Howard Hendricks wrote:

> Every man reading this book should seek to have three individuals in his life. You need a Paul. You need a Barnabas. You need a Timothy.[2]

While Promise Keepers is a ministry to men by men, this principle applies to everyone in the body of Christ (for example, see Titus 2:3-5). Dr. Hendricks encourages each believer to have a Paul in his life because "you need someone who's been down the road." Every believer needs a Barnabas because you need someone "who loves you but is not impressed by you." You also need a Timothy "into whose life you are building."[3] Servant leaders in team ministry need a mentor, a partner, and a protégé—someone they can train in servanthood. These people don't necessarily need to be on your ministry team, but they should be part of your ministry.

As a servant leader, you're a mentor, and you need a mentor. You're a mentor to those you lead. In addition, you need a mentor to show you how to lead. Mentoring is part of servant leadership because it's the way you prepare the next generation of leaders for service. Without future leaders there's no future.

Record the name of your mentor or potential mentor.

Record the name of someone you are mentoring or could mentor.

PERSONAL EVALUATION

Fill in the blanks with the words that represent TEAM ministry.

T _____

E _____

A _____

M _____

As you think about what you've studied this week and as you consider your ministry team, list some areas of need you might address in a team you're leading or would like to lead.

SUMMARY

- TEAM characteristic 4 is mentoring. Servant leaders are mentors to people who are working with them in team ministry.
- Mentoring is the way Christ's work is passed on to the next generation of servant leaders. To mentor is to multiply Christ and Kingdom ministry in the life of another person.
- Jesus mentored His disciples by teaching them and by demonstrating God's power in their lives.
- Paul was Timothy's mentor.
- Mentoring means taking what you've caught from your mentor and sharing it with another person.
- Servant leaders model for others what Christ modeled for them.
- Servant leaders in team ministry need a mentor, a partner, and a protégé—someone they can train in servanthood.
- You're a mentor and need a mentor in your ministry as a servant leader.

1. Theodore Wilhelm Engstrom and Paul A. Cedar, *Compassionate Leadership,* Kindle edition (Ventura, CA: Regal Books, 2006), 953.
2. Excerpt from *Seven Promises of a Promise Keeper* by Howard G. Hendricks. Edited and published by Focus on the Family. Copyright © 1994, Promise Keepers. All rights reserved. International copyright secured. Used by permission.
3. Ibid., 53–54.

Day 5
THE NEXT STEPS FOR A SERVANT LEADER

We tend to think we need leaders who serve,
but really we need servants who lead.[1]
NEIL COLE

Today You Will
- Complete your study of *Jesus on Leadership*.
- Learn four next steps to becoming a servant leader.
- Decide what you'll do to continue the process of becoming a servant leader.
- Spend time in prayer about servant leadership and team ministry.

You've almost completed this important study of servant leadership. Hopefully, you've been inspired as you studied Jesus' teachings and examples of servant leadership. You've been encouraged by seeing the way God has uniquely prepared you to serve Him. You've been challenged to equip someone for ministry and to team with others to reach a shared ministry goal. Now you may be asking, What do I do next? What do I do with all this information?

Let's spend today completing a plan to help you continue this journey of servant leadership. It will involve four steps:

Step 1. Make Jesus' model of servant leadership the pattern for the way you lead.

Step 2. Be alert to ways God is working in your life to mold you into a servant leader.

Step 3. Continue seeking ways to equip others for ministry.

Step 4. Team with others in ministry.

Step 1

MAKE JESUS' MODEL OF SERVANT LEADERSHIP THE PATTERN FOR THE WAY YOU LEAD.

Reflect on your journey through this study. In week 1 you experienced Jesus' teachings and examples of servant leadership. Jesus' messages and events in His life provided a completely new model of leadership for Jesus' disciples. This model must define the way you lead as a follower of Christ. To follow Jesus is to lead like Jesus.

So the first answer to your question, What do I do next? is to make Jesus' teachings and examples of servant leadership the benchmark for the way you lead others. This will require a process of transforming your thinking and behavior (see Rom. 12:2). You won't lead this way naturally. You must allow Jesus to be your Master Teacher on leadership. You must take steps to spend time with the Master so that He can empower you to lead as a servant leader.

Here are some suggestions to continue the process of following Jesus' servant-leadership model. Select the activities you'll do to continue learning to lead like Jesus.

____ **If I haven't already done so, I'll memorize Mark 10:45 and apply it to my daily decisions.**

____ **I'll memorize the seven principles of servant leadership or carry them with me each day.**

____ **I'll study and seek to lead by these four major passages of Scripture that describe how Jesus led as a servant: Mark 10:35-45; Luke 14:7-11; John 13:3-11; Philippians 2:5-11.**

____ **I'll invite a friend to learn and apply these principles with me.**

____ **I'll ask someone who's a servant leader, such as a pastor or another church leader, to continue to mentor me in this process.**

Step 2

BE ALERT TO WAYS GOD IS WORKING IN YOUR LIFE TO MOLD YOU INTO A SERVANT LEADER

In weeks 2–3 you considered ways God gifted you spiritually, used experiences to shape your witness, molded the way you relate to others, guided you to gain vocational skills, and enthused you with His Spirit for ministry. These insights resulted in your SERVE profile (see week 3, day 5). Believers' spiritual gifts, experiences, relational style, vocational skills, and enthusiasm are the tools of servant leadership that God uses to build the church. The church is the body of Christ, and you're an important member of that body. You're essential to the functioning of your local body of believers. All the other members are also essential. You alone don't have all the skills and gifts to carry out the mission of the church. The church functions best when it works like a body rather than an institution.

You must submit each part of who you are to Jesus' example. Otherwise, you've merely finished another exercise in self-discovery. Stay aware of ways God has worked and is continuing to work in your life. Allow the Holy Spirit to mold you into Jesus' model of servant leadership.

Ask yourself the following questions on a regular basis to be certain you're on the right track as you join God where He's working in your church and community.

- How can I use the spiritual gifts God has given me to serve Him and His church? Where can I use these gifts most effectively?
- How do my life experiences affect the way I see God, others, and myself? What's God doing in my life now to mold me into Christlikeness?
- How do my natural relational tendencies guide my behavior as a leader? In what ways must the Holy Spirit balance these tendencies to make me a stronger servant leader?
- How can I continually use my vocational skills as a servant leader? Am I learning new skills that I can implement in ministry?
- Whom can I equip to find a place of servant leadership in the church?
- Whom do I need to include on my ministry team who has a complementary SERVE profile?

Step 3

CONTINUE SEEKING WAYS TO EQUIP OTHERS FOR MINISTRY

Servant leaders equip others for ministry. Sometimes they do this by actively teaching and leading them. At other times they simply model a positive example of servant leadership. Leadership involves training those you lead so that they can serve effectively.

Below is a checklist of actions for intentionally seeking to equip others.

- Keep a prayer list of people you sense are ready to serve in ministry. Pray daily for those God wants you to equip for service. Ask Him, "Is this the person You want me to invest in and equip for ministry?"
- Regularly encourage people you're training. Write an email or send a small gift to let them know they're on the right track.
- Know a person's SERVE profile before you ask him or her to serve in a particular ministry. Ask yourself, *Do this person's gifts and abilities match the ministry I'm asking him or her to do?*
- Take time to listen to people you're equipping. Join them for lunch or invite them over for coffee. Also observe them while they serve to learn how you can help them.

- Encourage people you lead to continue growing in Christlikeness. What skills and attitudes must they learn to be effective in the ministry you've asked them to do?
- Pray often for people you're training. Without your prayers they're helpless to succeed in ministry.

Step 4

TEAM WITH OTHERS IN MINISTRY

This week you learned that leadership is a team sport. You learned that team ministry is the most effective means for servant leaders. Use these suggestions to begin building your ministry team.

- Remember that team ministry isn't a complicated process. It can involve a group of people who teach conversational English to international students, or it can involve teaching a group of people who teach preschoolers on Sunday morning. When your team has agreed on its goals, guide members into training opportunities that will enhance their gifts and abilities.
- Plan fellowship events to build a sense of togetherness on your team. Spend time as a group in prayer about the needs God wants you to work together to meet. With a Christlike spirit be prepared to address any sense that the team isn't together in direction or attitude. Listen to concerns and address needs to communicate that all members of the team are important.
- Make sure you've empowered your team with the authority and resources to reach the shared goals of the group. Team members must feel that they have the necessary skills and opportunities to carry out their tasks.
- Create an ongoing sense of accountability among the team members. Be open to share ways you have failed and ways you need their help to reach the team's goals. Build an understanding that each of you is accountable to God for the results of your ministry team.

PERSONAL EVALUATION

The process of becoming a servant leader is never finished. You've only begun this exciting journey. As you complete today's lesson, spend time in prayer. Consider the following two statements. Be prepared to share your commitments with your group.

I'll commit to continuing the process of becoming a servant leader by following the four suggested steps in this today's lesson.   Yes   No

As part of my role as a servant leader, I'll encourage others to participate in a study of *Jesus on Leadership.* I'll begin today praying for people God wants to mold into servant leaders for Kingdom ministry.   Yes   No

SUMMARY

The four suggested next steps in becoming a servant leader are:
1. Make Jesus' model of servant leadership the pattern for the way you lead.
2. Be alert to ways God is working in your life to mold you into a servant leader.
3. Continue seeking ways to equip others for ministry.
4. Team with others in ministry.

Your commitment to live out the principles in this study will affect the way you serve as a leader in your church or in the ministry to which God has called you.

You've completed this study of *Jesus on Leadership.* What one or two of the most significant truths have you learned from this study? Record them here and be prepared to share them in your next group session.

1. Neil Cole, *Organic Leadership: Leading Naturally Right Where You Are,* Kindle edition (Grand Rapids, MI: Baker Books, 2009), 2435–36.

LEADER GUIDE

Session 1
BECOMING A SERVANT LEADER

OVERVIEW
This session introduces the concept of servant leadership and need for servant leaders in the church. You'll introduce Jesus' teachings on servant leadership and overview the six-week study. To prepare to lead group sessions, complete the entire study before session 1.

SESSION GOALS
After this session participants should be able to—
- overview the study, using the three major concepts of SERVE, EQUIP, and TEAM;
- identify Scripture passages in which Jesus taught and modeled servant leadership;
- identify seven principles of servant leadership.

PLANNING FOR THE SESSION
1. Order a copy of *Jesus on Leadership* for each person.
2. If you're meeting in the church or a formal meeting room, you might want to set up tables so that participants will be able to use their Bible-study books and Bibles while taking notes easily. If possible, set up the tables and chairs so that each person can see the others in the group and can talk face-to-face. Another option is to meet informally in someone's home. The group could meet in one home throughout the study, or the group could meet in a different home each week.
3. Spend time praying for participants.
4. Have the title of the study displayed on a whiteboard as members enter the room.

DURING THIS SESSION
OPENING ACTIVITIES
1. As members arrive, welcome them and distribute Bible-study books. When it's time to begin, introduce yourself and share some information about yourself, such as the length of time you've been a member of the church and other areas in which you've served.
2. Ask members to share their names, the length of time they've been members of the church, and where they've served in the church in the past. After everyone has shared, tell members not to worry if they've never served in a leadership position before. One purpose of this study is to help them discover their places of service in the church.
3. Pause and pray for the group. Ask God to guide each person present as he or she considers a place of servant leadership.

4. Ask group members to play a word-association game, saying the first word that comes to mind when you give the following words: leader, *servant, great, head table, washing feet, waiting on tables, empowered, team.* Explain that each of these words is related in some way to Jesus' teachings on leadership. One goal of this study is to help participants understand and model servant leadership as Jesus did.

5. Ask a volunteer to read aloud Luke 14:7-11. Say: "Jesus taught His disciples to humble themselves, and He would exalt them. Too many times leaders seek the head table before the host invites them. In too many churches today head tables have replaced the towel and washbasin as symbols of leadership among God's people. Churches need leaders who step down from the head table and serve in the kitchen. Churches in the 21st century need men and women who won't follow the world's idea of leadership but who adopt Jesus' teachings and examples of servant leadership."

6. State: "Servant leadership is needed and will make a difference in the church today. During this study the group will search the Scriptures and your hearts to discover how God has already prepared you to be a servant leader in the church, in your community, and in your homes. You'll study Jesus' teachings and examples of servant leadership, ways God has prepared you to be a servant leader, how to equip others to join you in service, and how to team with others in ministry to multiply your leadership."

OVERVIEW THE STUDY

1. Say: "The purpose of this study is to help us discover, equip, and place servant leaders in all areas of ministry. In addition, this study can lead us, as members of the body of Christ, to discover our roles as servant leaders and can equip us for team ministry."

2. Ask members to turn to the core concepts of the study on pages 6–7. State: "Servant Leaders SERVE God and EQUIP Others for TEAM Ministry." Explain that SERVE, EQUIP, and TEAM are three acrostics that represent the servant-leadership principles that participants will study over the next weeks. As you briefly mention the components of each acrostic, you may want to write them on a whiteboard for emphasis.

PREVIEW WEEK 1

1. State that Jesus taught and modeled servant leadership. Ask volunteers to read aloud the seven principles of servant leadership on page 7, as well as the Scripture passages that relate to the principles.

2. Explain that this week participants will study these seven principles of servant leadership by completing personal reading assignments and learning activities. Ask them to complete week 1 in their workbooks before the next group session. Point out that each week's personal study is divided into five lessons labeled days 1–5. Encourage them to complete one lesson in a given day rather than all five lessons at once.

3. Direct members to the introduction to week 1. State that each week's study includes a memory verse that will teach them to follow Jesus' model of servant leadership. Encourage them to memorize each week's memory verse. Next week's verse is Mark 10:45.

CONCLUSION

Close in prayer that during the course of this study, God will teach the group more about servant leadership and will call members into the roles of service He's planned for them.

Session 2
DOWN FROM THE HEAD TABLE

OVERVIEW

You'll review what members experienced in their personal study this week as they learned ways Jesus taught and modeled servant leadership. You'll introduce them to the process that will lead each person to the completion of the SERVE profile at the end of week 3.

SESSION GOALS

After this session participants should be able to—
- summarize the seven principles of servant leadership;
- compose their own definitions of *servant leadership*;
- share their feelings about being a leader, as well as needs in their church and community that require servant leadership.

PLANNING FOR THE SESSION

1. Have poster paper, felt-tip pens, and masking tape available for a small-group activity.
2. Spend time praying for participants.
3. Memorize this week's memory verse, Mark 10:45.

DURING THIS SESSION
OPENING ACTIVITIES

1. As members arrive, ask them to form pairs and complete the statement "My most respected leader is …" After everyone has had a chance to share, ask: "How has your understanding of Jesus as a leader changed after this week of study?"
2. Ask a volunteer to quote this week's memory verse, Mark 10:45. State that this is the foundational verse for *Jesus on Leadership*. Jesus not only taught His disciples about servant leadership but also modeled it for them, giving His life so that others could live.

3. Pause and pray for the group, asking for God's wisdom and insight as members share what God has shown them this week about Jesus' example as a servant leader.

REVIEW WEEK 1

1. Divide participants into small groups of three or four persons each. Give each group a large sheet of paper, a felt-tip pen, and masking tape. Ask each group to write a definition or a description of *servant leadership,* based on their study of week 1. When everyone has finished, ask a member of each group to tape its definition to a wall and to present the definition.

2. Review the four key elements of Jesus' leadership in week 1, day 5. Emphasize that as servant leaders, we're to follow His example.

3. Say: "No one can be a servant without a master. You can't be a servant leader as modeled by Jesus without having Him as your Master." Ask a volunteer to read Matthew 6:24. Then continue: "Leaders without Jesus as their Master can serve only themselves, not others. The only possibility for you to know the servant leadership of Jesus is to make Him the Master of your life and commit to follow His teachings and His examples." State that after this session you'll be glad to talk with anyone who wants to know more about making Jesus the Master of his or her life.

4. Direct members to page 7 and remind them that they studied seven principles of servant leadership this week. Say: "In day 1 you examined servanthood leadership principle 1, based on Luke 14:7-11." Ask someone to read principle 1 aloud.

5. Say: "In day 2 you observed Jesus' teachings about greatness and being first from Mark 10:35-45. What was James and John's request?" Ask a member to read servant leadership principle 2. Say: "Servant leadership isn't about position and power. It's about following Jesus. What was the response of the other 10 disciples to James and John?" Ask someone to read verse 42. Does this happen in our world? Jesus said the world's way isn't to be the way among His followers." Read verse 43a.

6. Ask a volunteer to read Mark 10:43b-44 and servant leadership principle 3. Ask members to turn to "Personal Evaluation" at the end of week 1, day 2 and to share the honest thoughts and feelings they recorded in their personal study.

7. Read John 13:3 and list the statements that describe what Jesus knew about Himself at this time. Discuss these statements. Ask members to share the ways they rated their trust in God in week 1, day 3. Read servant leadership principle 4.

8. Read John 13:4-11. Describe what Jesus did. Review the material in "The Ministry of the Towel" in week 1, day 3. Read servant leadership principle 5. Say: "Those who lead in God's kingdom lead from a kneeling position, dressed like a servant, meeting the needs of those who follow them." Ask: "How can you 'wash the feet' of people you know?" List responses on a whiteboard. Encourage members to make these ideas actual habits in their relationships with others.

9. Read servant leadership principle 6. State: "The disciples modeled this principle in the early church. The seventh principle is a story from the life of Moses." Read servant leadership principle 7.

10. Ask volunteers to identify servant-leadership principles that seem to be a part of their lives today. Then ask them to identify Scripture passages they studied this week that taught them the most about servant leadership.

11. Ask members to share in pairs their honest feelings about being a leader, the needs they feel their church needs to address, and people they could ask to join them in meeting those needs. Then the pairs should pray for each other, asking God to encourage them to lead and meet needs in the church and community.

PREVIEW WEEK 2

1. Direct members to the SERVE acrostic on page 6. Say: "You've committed to being a servant leader as Jesus taught and modeled among His followers. The next step in becoming a servant leader is discovering how God has prepared you for service through the ways He's designed and gifted you. In this week's personal study you'll discover and learn about your spiritual gifts and the experiences God has used to mold you into the leader He wants you to be." Ask members to complete week 2 in their workbooks before the next group session, including the spiritual-gifts inventory and scoring.

2. Ask a volunteer to read next week's Scripture-memory verse, 1 Peter 4:10. Explain that this verse reminds us that the gifts God has given us are for His glory. Servant leaders have the privilege of administering God's grace shown to us through Jesus Christ.

CONCLUSION

Close by praying that members will better understand how God has equipped them to be servant leaders as they discover their spiritual gifts and consider their formative experiences this week.

Session 3
LEADERS WHO SERVE, PART 1

OVERVIEW

You'll review what group members experienced in their personal study this week as they examined biblical concepts of the church and spiritual gifts. You'll also review the idea that God uses experiences to lead believers to places of servant leadership. You'll lead participants to understand how these aspects of a person's life relate to servant leadership.

SESSION GOALS

After this session participants should be able to—

- share whether they see their accomplishments as profit or loss;
- characterize the nature of the church;
- share their own definitions of *spiritual gifts;*
- share the spiritual gifts they've discovered in their lives;
- share their spiritual markers and timelines with the group.

PLANNING FOR THE SESSION

1. Draw these diagrams on a whiteboard or on a poster.

   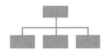

2. Spend time praying for participants.
3. Memorize this week's memory verse, 1 Peter 4:10.

DURING THIS SESSION

OPENING ACTIVITIES

1. As members enter, ask them to decide which diagram best represents church. Then ask them to share why they chose this symbol. There are no right or wrong answers. All of them reflect aspects of the church. After several members have shared their responses, say: "We all come to church with our own impressions of what it should be. I hope this week's study helped you see the church and your place in it in a different light."
2. Ask a volunteer to quote this week's memory verse, 1 Peter 4:10.
3. Pause and pray for the group, asking God to guide members as they share ways He's worked in their lives to prepare them for servant leadership.

REVIEW WEEK 2

1. Ask members to refer to the SERVE acrostic in week 2, day 1 as you describe each element. State: "God uses your relationship with Christ, as well as these five areas of your life, as the raw materials to mold you into a servant leader. This week you studied the nature of the church. You also learned about spiritual gifts and identified ways God has worked in your life to prepare you to serve."
2. Ask participants to share their own definitions of *spiritual gift.* Use the material in week 2, day 2 to provide a biblical definition.

3. Ask: "What's the purpose of spiritual gifts?" After a brief discussion, provide answers from week 2, day 2, based on 1 Corinthians 12:7 and Ephesians 4:12.

4. Discuss the two attitudes that can prevent people from feeling they're part of the church's mission ("I don't belong" and "I don't need you"). Use Paul's teachings in 1 Corinthians 12:14-26 to show the error of these feelings.

5. Say: "God has given each of you spiritual gifts for service in and through Christ's body, the church. Servant leaders lead by Spirit-empowered service." Ask participants to share the gifts they discovered by completing the spiritual-gifts inventory this week.

6. State: "This week we also looked at our experiences God has used to mold us into servant leaders. Share personal experiences from your lives that illustrate ways God uses experiences to mold believers into servant leaders."

7. Ask members to turn to the timelines they created in week 2, day 5. Instruct them to form small groups of two or three and to share their timelines and a spiritual marker when God changed their lives forever.

PREVIEW WEEK 3

1. Refer again to the SERVE acrostic in week 2, day 1. Say: "This week you'll study three other areas of your life that God uses to mold you into His servant leader: your relational style, your vocational skills, and your God-given enthusiasm for ministry." Ask members to complete week 3 before the next group session, including the relational survey.

2. Ask a volunteer to read next week's Scripture-memory verse, 2 Corinthians 12:9, which records Paul's confession of total dependency on Christ as his source of strength. Say: "As you discover how God has prepared you to be a servant leader, remember that you're effective only when you depend on God and His strength rather than your own."

CONCLUSION

Close by praying that members will start seeing the way God has designed them to be servant leaders as they focus on relational style, vocational skills, and enthusiasm this week.

Session 4
LEADERS WHO SERVE, PART 2

OVERVIEW

You'll review what group members experienced in their personal study this week. You'll survey the four relational styles, how vocational skills can be used for service, and the personal enthusiasm God gives believers for His purposes.

SESSION GOALS

After this session participants should be able to—
- share their predominant relational style;
- share their vocational skills that can be used in service to God;
- share their enthusiasm for ministry;
- share their SERVE profiles with the group.

PLANNING FOR THE SESSION

1. Write the following names on a whiteboard or on a poster: Paul, Barnabas, Abraham, Moses.
2. You'll need felt-tip pens, masking tape, and poster paper for a small-group activity.
3. Spend time praying for participants.
4. Memorize this week's memory verse, 2 Corinthians 12:9.

DURING THIS SESSION

OPENING ACTIVITIES

1. Ask members to turn to the SERVE acrostic on page 6. Say: "Last week you examined spiritual gifts and experiences to begin understanding your servant-leadership profile. This week you studied relational styles, vocational skills, and enthusiasm for ministry. These are three more areas of your life that God uses to make you a servant leader."
2. Ask a volunteer to quote this week's memory verse, 2 Corinthians 12:9. Say: "In this verse Paul confessed that whenever he found himself weak, God was powerful. Paul had a strong personality. This verse is an example of how a dominant relational style submits to the power of God over the power of self."
3. Pause and pray for the group, asking God to guide members as they continue discovering the way God has wired them for servant leadership among His people.

REVIEW WEEK 3

1. Ask participants to read the names you've written on a whiteboard or on a poster. Ask them to form four small groups according to the biblical character they most closely identified with in their relational surveys. Say: "Each person in your small group has a similar relational style that impacts each person's servant leadership. Discuss the person from the Bible whose style is similar to your own. Share your answers to the questions in week 3, day 2 about this biblical personality, as well as what you see as his strengths and weaknesses. How do they compare with members of your small group?"
2. Review the two words of caution related to natural behavioral styles in week 3, day 1. Stress that God's Spirit within us, producing His fruit, is the way God completes who we are as His creation. Say: "God's Holy Spirit is the perfect balance to our natural

relational styles. Sometimes we face conflict with others because of relationship styles. This can cause division in the body. We learned from our study of the nature of the church that God intends the church to be unified." Ask a volunteer to read Colossians 3:12-14. Ask: "What clothing are we to wear as chosen children of God? What should be our standard of forgiveness? What's the virtue that binds all these together in unity?" State: "As a servant leader, you should be sensitive to a person's relational needs and serve him by loving and forgiving as Christ loved and forgave you."

3. Explain: "Your relational style will help you choose your role as a servant leader. God made you in a special way for His purposes. There's no other person in the world like you." Ask: "What did the relational survey tell you about yourself that you weren't aware of? Why is it important to talk about relational style when discussing servant leadership?" Allow time to discuss the survey result and its relationship to servant leadership.

4. Say: "Now let's look at ways we can use our vocational skills for God's glory." Ask members to form two small groups and to turn to week 3, day 3. Ask one group to share their answers about Moses and Simon Peter. Ask the other group to share their answers about Paul and Lydia. Say: "God has called people with different kinds of vocational skills to do His work. The job they do is secondary to what they do for God." Ask: "What two vocational skills did Paul have? How did God use these in Paul's life?"

5. Ask members to share in their small groups their responses to the activities in "My Vocational Skills" and "My Skills for Gods' Calling" in week 3, day 4. Give each group a felt-tip pen and poster paper and ask them to compile one list of all the skills represented by their group. When each group has finished, tape their list to a wall where everyone can see them. Ask: "What comes to mind as you look at these lists?" Allow time for responses. Summarize by stating: "Imagine what God could do in our church and community if we unconditionally gave Him each of these skills for His purposes."

6. Introduce God-given enthusiasm for ministry as another aspect of our lives that God uses to mold us for His service. Ask participants to complete this statement: "The one thing I do for God that makes my heart beat fast is …"

7. Ask members to share the results of the SERVE profiles they completed in week 3, day 5. After everyone has shared, ask: "What do these profiles say about you and other members of the group? How does this knowledge help you as a servant leader? Would this information be helpful to those who recruit workers in our church?"

PREVIEW WEEK 4

1. Direct members to the EQUIP acrostic on page 6. Say: "Servant leaders equip others to help them meet needs. This week's study is about how to equip others for service." Ask members to complete week 4 in their workbooks before the next group session.

2. Ask a volunteer to read next week's Scripture-memory verses, Ephesians 4:11-12. Explain that part of a servant leader's job is to equip others for service.

CONCLUSION

Close in prayer, thanking God for the ways He's prepared each member for service. Pray for wisdom and strength to serve where He's called each member to serve. Ask Him to show members the people they should encourage to join them in ministry as they learn how to equip others for ministry this week.

Session 5
HOW TO EQUIP OTHERS

OVERVIEW

You'll review what group members experienced in their personal study this week as they learned five steps for equipping others for ministry. You'll guide members in how to seek people to join them in ministry.

SESSION GOALS

After this session participants should be able to—
- recall how Jesus encouraged His disciples and how Barnabas encouraged Saul to join him in ministry;
- describe how Jesus qualified those who wanted to follow Him;
- share what they believe to be the best ways to observe the needs of others;
- identify ways Jesus instructed His disciples and ways Paul taught Timothy to equip him for ministry;
- state the value of praying for those they seek to equip for service.

PLANNING FOR THE SESSION

1. Arrange the chairs in small groups so that members can form groups as they enter. Place a sheet of poster paper, a felt-tip pen, and masking tape in the center of each circle.
2. Spend time praying for participants.
3. Memorize this week's memory verses, Ephesians 4:11-12.

DURING THIS SESSION

OPENING ACTIVITIES

1. Read the following case study to the group: "John is a leader in his church. He's served for several years, but lately he's become discouraged. He feels that people can never get along. He's not sure he's qualified to do the job he's been asked to do. He's lost his

enthusiasm for ministry and isn't sure he even knows how to do the work his pastor has asked him to do. His discouragement has brought him to the place that he even doubts God's presence in his life."

2. Say: "John is like many church leaders. He's served a long time, but no one seems to have encouraged and helped him as a leader. Your instructions are to use what you've learned this week about equipping others to help John get back on track with his ministry. List five actions you'd take to help John. You'll have five minutes. When you've finished, tape your suggestions to a wall so that everyone can see them."

3. When the groups have finished, point out the EQUIP acrostic on page 6. Ask a member of each group to report and show how their list fits into the acrostic.

4. Say: "Part of our role as servant leaders is to encourage and equip others for service, as our Scripture-memory verses this week remind us". Ask a volunteer to quote Ephesians 4:11-12. Explain that God gave the church different kinds of gifts to carry out different functions. The purpose of those gifts is "for the training of the saints in the work of ministry, to build up the body of Christ" (v. 12).

5. Pause and pray for the group, asking God to guide members as they seek people they can equip for ministry in God's kingdom.

REVIEW WEEK 4

1. Ask members to identify the first step to EQUIP others for service. Briefly discuss encouraging others to serve. Ask members to identify ways Jesus encouraged His disciples from week 4, day 1.

2. Ask: "How did Barnabas encourage Saul to join him in ministry?" Instruct members to divide into small groups and to identify one person who's been a "Barnabas" in their lives, someone who encouraged them to get involved in ministry. Then ask them to share the names of one or two people they want to encourage to join them in ministry and why.

3. Ask someone to share the two ways servant leaders qualify those they equip from week 4, day 2. Read aloud the paragraph in week 4, day 2 beginning, "At the same time, keep in mind that no one is perfect." Encourage members to find a balance between standards that are too high and no standards at all.

4. Ask: "How did Jesus qualify people who wanted to follow Him? What did Paul teach Timothy about persons to whom he should entrust the gospel?" See week 4, day 2.

5. Ask participants to turn in their workbooks to week 4, day 3. Ask them to share their responses to the activity asking them to identify what they believe to be the best way to observe someone and understand his or her need. Ask: "What are two ways you can understand the needs of people you equip?"

6. Read the case study in "How Can You Instruct Others?" in week 4, day 4. Ask: "How would you instruct Steve and help him become successful in this ministry?"

7. Ask a volunteer to read John 17:6-19. Ask members to describe how Jesus' prayer for His disciples makes them feel. Say: "Jesus prayed for His disciples, and Paul asked Christians to pray for him. Servant leaders pray for those they equip for ministry."

8. Read the paragraph in week 4, day 5 that begins, "No servant leader should stand to lead until he kneels to pray with those he serves."

9. Ask members to reform their small groups and share the way they completed "My EQUIP Progress" at the end of week 4, day 5.

PREVIEW WEEK 5

1. Direct members to pages 6–7. State: "We've learned that servant leaders SERVE God and EQUIP others to serve. This week we'll see that servant leaders also serve in TEAM ministry." Ask members to complete week 5 in their workbooks before the next group session.

2. Ask a volunteer to read next week's Scripture-memory verse, Mark 6:7.

3. Ask members to contact one person this week they'd like to join them in ministry. Ask members also to prayerfully consider seeking spiritual mentors to equip them in their roles as servant leaders.

CONCLUSION

Close in prayer, asking God to teach each member the power of prayer and the joy of equipping others in ministry. Ask Him to lead members to other believers they can team with to multiply their ministry.

Session 6
HOW TO SERVE IN TEAM MINISTRY

OVERVIEW

You'll review what members experienced in their personal study this week and introduce them to the concept of TEAM ministry. You'll bring the study to a close and encourage participants to continue seeking God's calling for them as servant leaders.

SESSION GOALS

After this session participants should be able to—
- recall their best experiences of being involved with a team;
- define *team ministry;*
- state the four components of TEAM ministry;

- share their personal evaluation from each day's lesson related to the four components of TEAM ministry;
- share the names of their mentors, partners, and protégés;
- share the two most meaningful elements of their study of *Jesus on Leadership*.

PLANNING FOR THE SESSION

1. You'll need poster paper, felt-tip pens, and masking tape for a small-group activity.
2. Arrange the chairs in circles forming four small groups. Tape a sheet of poster paper to a wall near each group. Each group will also need a felt-tip pen.
3. Spend time praying for participants.
4. Memorize this week's memory verse, Mark 6:7.

DURING THIS SESSION

OPENING ACTIVITIES

1. As members enter, ask them to join a small group and identify on the poster paper a team they've been part of that was meaningful to them—a sports team, a management team, or even their marriage. Then ask members to explain their answers. After everyone has shared, say: "Leadership is a team sport. Servant leaders know they're most effective when they team with others to meet a shared goal. Today we'll review what you've learned about team ministry. The purpose of this study is for you to become a servant leader in team ministry. Servant leaders serve best when they serve with others."
2. Ask a volunteer to quote this week's memory verse, Mark 6:7. Point out that Jesus spent three years equipping His disciples to continue His ministry after He was gone.
3. Pause and pray for the group, asking God to guide members as they seek to understand and live out servant leadership in team ministry.

REVIEW WEEK 5

1. Refer members to the TEAM acrostic on page 7. Say: "Team ministry is a group of disciples bound together under the lordship of Christ who are committed to the shared goal of meeting a particular need. An important aspect of this definition is the phrase *bound together*. What are some things that bind team members together?"
2. While members are still in four small groups, assign each group one component of the acrostic TEAM: togetherness (week 5, day 1), empowerment (day 2), accountability (day 3), or mentoring (day 4). Instruct each group to review the appropriate day's lesson in week 5 and to summarize the assigned component of the acrostic. Tell the groups to include the following points.